Theodora M. L Lane-Clarke

Roman violets : and where they blossom

Theodora M. L Lane-Clarke

Roman violets : and where they blossom

ISBN/EAN: 9783741175633

Manufactured in Europe, USA, Canada, Australia, Japa

Cover: Foto ©Andreas Hilbeck / pixelio.de

Manufactured and distributed by brebook publishing software (www.brebook.com)

Theodora M. L Lane-Clarke

Roman violets : and where they blossom

ROMAN VIOLETS,

And where they Blossom.

BY

THEODORA M. L. LANE-CLARKE.

> 'There are buds that fold within them,
>   Close and covered from our sight,
> Many a richly-tinted petal
>   Never looked on by the light :
> Fain to see their shrouded faces,
>   Sun and dew are long at strife,
> Till at length the sweet buds open—
>   Such a bud is life.'   JEAN INGELOW.

LONDON: BURNS & OATES.
1879.

CONTENTS.

CHAP.		PAGE
I.	'Hath Fortune smiled on us?'	1
II.	The Magician	19
III.	On the Blue Sea	30
IV.	The Destined Haven	37
V.	What old Simpole said	49
VI.	'Poor Bobbie!'	57
VII.	One Saturday Afternoon	64
VIII.	An Empty Cage	72
IX.	The Fairy Godmother	80
X.	A long Talk	88
XI.	Is he Dead?	98
XII.	Visiting-day at the Hospital	107
XIII.	Another Visitor	114
XIV.	Two little Red Riding-hoods	122
XV.	Where is Nanna?	130
XVI.	Christmas in the Wards	138
XVII.	Cesare's Vocation	146
XVIII.	'To be, or not to be'	153
XIX.	'Et après?'	161
XX.	Another Eastertide	168
XXI.	Will he come?	177

ROMAN VIOLETS.

CHAPTER I.

'HATH FORTUNE SMILED ON US?'

IT was a sunny morning in Rome. Eastertide, the busiest season of the year, had brought strangers from all parts to witness the great Paschal ceremonies, and a very Babel of conflicting tongues flowed unceasingly from the Pincio to St. Peter's, from the old Flaminian Gate to the ruins of the Colosseum. Two children, barefooted, hand in hand, ran across the great Piazza del Popolo, on which the sun was streaming down fiercely enough, even at that early hour, and paused where three long busy streets carried the traffic of the town in divergent lines to south and east and west.

'Shall we go down the Corso or the Babuino, Cesare?' says the smaller one, a girl of about nine years old, with torn and dirty brown skirt, and black bodice fastened over what had once been a white chemisette, though now so grimy as to be almost indistinguishable.

The boy is a bright, black-eyed, brown-skinned little fellow, clothed in a nondescript kind of shirt, open at the neck, and very short in the arms, with pantaloons of the same material, reaching to the knee, whence his little bare legs, thin and brown as sticks, were the only continuations.

In his hand is a great dewy bunch of fresh violets, neatly tied together with a bit of ribbon; and the girl holds a basket full of the same fragrant flowers, carefully shaded from the sun by large leaves, which she lifts now and then to peep at her treasures.

'I think the Via Babuino is the best,' he answers, looking down it as he speaks with anxious gravity; 'it is the street of the Inglesi, and they are so fond of flowers. Why, all the flower-shops are there, you know.'

'That is just why I am not sure of its being the best,' answers Nanna, hesitating; 'for of course if they can buy violets in the shops, they will not care to take ours.'

'We must run after them and tease them, until they give us a solde to get rid of us, as Rita does,' laughs Cesare, showing all his white teeth in malicious glee. 'Come, Nanna, do let us try the Inglesi to-day; and if they fail we will take the Corso to-morrow.'

'Very well,' she assents; and the two run off for their first essay in street-selling.

'Look, Nanna; I am going to speak to those ladies across the road;' and he is over in a minute, training his small voice to the whine of a professed beggar.

'O dear ladies, charity, charity! Only four soldi for these beautiful violets! Do buy a bunch of violets!'

'O, they are beauties!' laughs an English girl, stooping to inhale their fragrance; 'so fresh, too, with all the dew still on them! How much do you ask?' she questions, taking out her purse.

Quick-witted Cesare seizes the opportunity, like a true Italian.

'*Six* soldi a bunch, dear lady; only six!'

'O, I think it is too much, is it not, Kate? I never heard of such a price. Six soldi! Why that is threepence! Threepence for one bunch!'

'Of course it is too much. Don't you know

that they always ask just double what they will take? Offer him three, and come on quickly, or we shall never get to the Capitol.'

'Well, I will give you three soldi,' says the young lady, looking longingly at the violets.

'Impossible, signorina,' says cunning Cesare. 'My poor mother is ill at home; we have no bread to eat, and—'

'O, very well; then I will not have them;' and she walks on fast down the street.

'Ah, dear signorina, do take my violets!' he calls out, running beside her. 'See, what will you give me for them? I will take *five* soldi.'

'I have said *three*,' persists the young lady, without looking round.

'Ah, dear lady, for the sake of the poor mother at home, give me *four!*'

'Well, four, then, and give me that big bunch.' And she pours the coppers into his outstretched palm, leaving him radiant with delight.

Meanwhile, Nanna has been pursuing her prey with equal ardour on the other side of the street.

'Well, what have you done?' asks Cesare, dancing up to her.

'Sold two bunches, and got three soldi for each of them.'

'And I have got four for my one bunch,' he nods triumphantly ; 'that is better than you, eh, Nanna? Here, give me some more.' And he thrusts his hand into the basket.

'Get along, you little wretch!' she screams, pushing him off the pavement. 'What! I have all the trouble of carrying the basket, and you will come and jeer at me, will you, because you get one poor solde more than me? Go and gather flowers for yourself. Via!' And she stamps her foot at him.

'O dear Nanna, do not be angry. Here, I will give you the solde all for your own self, only let me have some more flowers.'

Nanna takes the money sulkily, tossing him two bunches, and they walk along in silence.

'How hard life is!' thinks the boy, as his little bare feet patter along the rough pavement. Not that he minds this physical hardness, however, having never known what it is to feel a bit of shoe-leather between him and the stones. Mother Nature has made his skin as tough and hard as are the kid boots of a London fine lady, and his warm Italian blood courses swiftly through his veins, defying the sharp east wind. What he does mind is the ill-temper of his little companion, for he is of a tender nature, and lives as truly in the light of others' smiles as any poet of his nation.

'I wish I knew how to please her,' he says to himself. 'If I don't sell my violets she will be cross, and yet she does not like me to get a halfpenny more than herself. She wants all the glory, and all the money too.'

Fortunately, however, for the little philosopher, Nanna presently gets a run of good fortune; and before the midday Angelus has rung from Sant' Andrea delle Fratte, her basket is empty, and her pocket quite weighty with coppers.

'Now we can make a festa,' she says, her eyes sparkling with glee. 'What shall we do?'

'O, let us get some white bread, and go and eat it by the fountain in the piazza there.'

'Yes, and see whether Bicè has earned anything too, little idle thing.'

So they count their halfpence, and expend three copper pieces in dainty *brioches*, a white cake-like bread after which Cesare's mouth has watered many and many a time as he passed that baker's shop in the Babuino, without the wherewithal to make one of them his own; and then they saunter up the street, nibbling at the bread as at something almost too good for everyday food, and reach the long flight of steps leading up to the Trinità di Monte, where the models sit in picturesque costumes and groups, waiting to be hired.

'There is Bicè!' cries Cesare, signalling to a girl on the topmost step, dressed in gayest Roman dress of green skirt, crimson apron bordered with embroideries of many colours, white chemisette turned back to show the brown throat circled with rows upon rows of coloured beads, and a light handkerchief folded square and laid upon her head. She flies down to them like a bright bird, her long gilt earrings flashing in the sun.

'O, you have sold your flowers! And got white bread for dinner! Do give me a little bit, I am so hungry, and no one has hired me.'

'Here, come and eat it with us by the fountain.' And the three children scramble up to the stone edge of the basin, and sit there, laughing and eating, catching the spray in their hands as it falls, and drinking it like birds, or splashing one another with silvery drops. Then they pour out their gains and count them over. 'And you have nothing? Poor Bicè!'

'No, I have nothing to day. But when I *do* get anything, it is always *silver !*' she says, holding her head proudly. 'And I have been much admired to-day, which is almost as good as one of your soldi. There came some *forestieri* (strangers) up the steps, and they all stood and looked at me, O, so long, and talked together. I could not understand what they said ; but one turned to the others and pointed at me and nodded, and another asked my name.'

'Perhaps they will hire you another day,' says Cesare hopefully, 'and then you will give us a treat of white bread too, will you not ?'

'Yes,' answers Bicè, somewhat reluctantly, for she dearly loved to spend her stray farthings on herself; 'but let us go home now.' And so the three children turn their steps towards home.

Bicè and Nanna live in a little narrow dirty crooked street, a long way from that bright square and cool fountain where they ate their dinner at noonday. They are sisters, although so unlike one another ; and poor little Cesare is an orphan, taken in by their father out of charity, in a fit of impulsive generosity, of which he has never heard the last from his indignant spouse, who is now standing at the door of their home, a high dilapidated-looking house, with small many-paned and barred windows, each room in which shelters a whole family. The Italian poor, however, live more constantly in the open air than the English, and therefore do not need much accommodation in the way of houseroom. Nothing is more common than to see whole families grouped together on every doorstep down the street; the mother or grandmother occupying the place of honour, a wooden chair in the midst, busily plying needle or distaff; an elder girl, perhaps, bending over her lace-cushion, while another nurses the baby; and the men sauntering up and down with pipes in their mouths, ready to answer all reproaches with, 'No man hath hired us.'

'Well, children,' calls the mother, as she catches sight of them, and suspends her work for an instant to fan herself vigorously with the large green-paper fan hung at her side, 'what have you got?'

'All this, mother!' And Nanna pours the coppers into her mother's lap.

Nita's fierce black eyes brighten at the sight.

'That is well done, Nanna. And you, Bicè?'

'I have nothing,' the little girl answers sulkily, hanging her head.

'Ah, you idle creature! you have been playing in the gutters instead of showing yourself on the piazza. Go; you shall have no dinner to-day. And you, Nanna and Cesare, here is some soup for you.'

'We bought some white bread with three of the coppers, mother, and ate it by the fountain,' puts in Nanna timidly.

'O you stupid!' whispers Bicè, pinching her arm; 'now you will not get any soup.'

But the mother is too much surprised by this extraordinary piece of truth-telling to give any answer until she has picked out from a dark corner a little bundle, which she hands over to Bicè.

'There; take the baby and go out.' And she pushes her into the street and shuts the door.

'Now, Nanna and Cesare, listen to me. When you sell your flowers you are to bring me every halfpenny you get, straight. When you are very good, I may give you a solde for yourselves now and then, but you are to bring it all here first. Do you hear? And take care you do not cheat me. I shall find out. Now, if you have finished your dinner, be off, and do not let me see you until bedtime.'

The children hastily swallow their remaining mouthfuls, and turn out again into the street. Bicè is waiting for them a little way off, crouching upon a doorstep, with the baby asleep in her arms.

'Now what shall we do this afternoon? We have ever so much time before sunset. Only you have had no soup, Bicè; and mother did not give us bread, so I could not bring you any.'

'Well, let us go and look at the great grand shops in the Corso, and pretend that we are going to buy gold necklaces and bracelets, and choose which we should like.'

'O no! Do come up the hill and see the fine carriages and horses,' pleads Cesare.

'Shops are better,' says Nanna decidedly. 'I do not like seeing the fine ladies, because I always want to be like them; but if we only look in at shop-windows, we can really quite pretend that we are going to buy them. This morning, as I stood close to a young lady who was looking into the jeweller's window in the great square, her mother said, "Now, my dear, you may buy anything you like which does not cost more than 300 francs,* but I cannot give you more." Well, she just cried, "O mother, the only thing I care for there is 400 francs, and I will not have anything else." So, you see, it was no use her having all that money to spend, because she only wanted one thing, and that one she could not have.'

'Ah, but if any one offered *me* 300 francs,' returns Bicè indignantly, 'I should know very well how to spend it, and say, "Thank you!" for it.'

'Yes. What would you buy?' says little Cesare, with wondering eyes.

'I should buy a beautiful silk dress—like that lady we saw one day going into Piale's shop. Do you remember, Nanna? And a white-lace bonnet, and plenty of gold chains and jewels; so that everybody would admire me, and want to paint me.'

'But I thought they liked our Roman dress best, Bicè? You know you always have to wear it.'

'Yes, indeed; I cannot think why they like it. Ugly old thing! I would never see it again if I could help it.'

* About 12*l*.

'O Bicè, I am sure you look very pretty in it!'

'Perhaps I do, Cesare; but that is because I am pretty. Not like that little frog Nanna, so thin and white.'

'I cannot help being ugly,' says Nanna, rather crossly; but she is too well accustomed to her vain little sister's unkind remarks to resent them, though she does long sometimes for the other's good looks.

Presently, looking down one of the little back streets which branch off here and there from the busy Corso, they catch sight of a tempting-looking group of children, and a tall man in their midst with a very battered old hat and shabby coat, evidently exhibiting something of unusual interest to the breathlessly-attentive little gathering.

'O Nanna, do let us go and see!' exclaims Cesare; and the three children advance towards the group.

'What is it, Sandra?' whispers Bicè to an acquaintance among the crowd.

'O, wonderful things! The gentleman is a magician. See that ugly little figure of a man with his mouth open which he has before him?

You put in your finger and thumb and pull out a paper, and there upon it is written everything about your own life—when you are going to be married, and to whom ; how many children you will have; at what age you will die ; and, in fact, all sorts of things.'

'And all that for nothing?' gasps Cesare ; while the others are too much overcome with awe to utter a word.

'O, of course you give a solde.'

'O dear!' groan all three at once ; 'we have not got any money. Have you, Sandra?'

'Yes ; I have just one solde, and I am going to give it. Now listen !'

And they listen, while the man pours out a long stream of invitations and explanations. ' Who wants his fortune told ? Who wishes to know if she will have a rich husband, and gold and silver in plenty ? Who seeks to learn his fate in this world, and the many or few years he has to live ? Now, my little maid'—this to Sandra, who stands irresolute—'do you want a *buona fortuna ?*'

'Yes, please, sir.'

'Come, then ; pull it out. Only one, remember ; so be careful. If you take two, you forfeit both.'

Sandra cautiously draws a long folded paper from the open mouth, and retires to the outskirts of the crowd to examine it at ease, Nanna, Bicè, and Cesare pressing round her. She reads it aloud:

'" Little girl,"' it began—('Ah, you see, it was meant for me,' remarks Sandra, in high delight.)—'" You are poor at present, and lead an unhappy life"—(That is very true.)—" But be patient; better times are at hand. No change will come to you until the age of twenty-three; but after that time you will be wooed by a rich and noble gentleman, who, after overcoming many obstacles, will at last succeed in making you his bride. You will then lead a happy life, and have five children, the eldest of whom will be in danger of dying by water. You will have several illnesses, especially one very bad one at about the age of fifty-eight, but you will not die of it. Your death will occur at the age of seventy-one."'

'O Sandra, how nice!' cry all the children, as she folds up the paper, her face beaming with delight.

'But what a long time to wait!' says Sandra, rather mournfully. 'Why, I am only nine now; so I must go on working for fourteen years.'

'Well, and we may go on all our lives,' sighs Bicè. 'I would not mind anything, if only I knew that I should be rich some day.'

'O, how I wish I had a solde!' says Cesare, half crying. 'I do so want to know my fortune too!'

'I have thought of something!' cries Nanna; and she quickly pushes her way to the man, who is still dispensing his bits of paper. 'Please, sir, I want a "good fortune" so much, but I have not any money to-day. Will you give me one now, and let me bring you the first of my earnings to-morrow? I sell violets in the streets; and I shall be sure to have plenty of soldi.'

'O no, indeed!' answers the man crossly. 'I shall be far enough away from this street to-morrow. Why, I am never two days in the same place.'

'But I would find you out; indeed I would,' pleads the little girl, clinging desperately to hope, though half wondering at her own temerity.

'No, no; move off!' and he pushes her rudely aside.

'Well, look here,' says Sandra, who has listened sympathisingly to poor Nanna's little attempt; 'just earn your money to-morrow morning, and then hunt up this man. He is sure to be somewhere near, in spite of what he says.'

'But I never saw him before: how can I be sure of finding him again? Besides,' says Nanna, growing more and more desponding, 'mother said we were not to spend any of the money.'

'We will ask her for a solde each, and promise to be very good afterwards,' suggests Cesare.

'Or keep back three soldi when we give her the money; she will never find out,' says Bicè.

Cesare is just opening his mouth to cry, 'For shame!' when he is touched on the shoulder by a man somewhat like the 'magician' who sold the paper fortunes, dressed in seedy black, with a very cross and repulsively-dirty face, which he tries in vain to twist into a pleasing smile.

'Come here, little boy; I want to speak to you;' and he draws the child aside, and asks him a few questions about his name and age and where he lives, to which Cesare replies in great bewilderment.

'So you would like to have your fortune told, eh? Well, *I* am a magician too, and perhaps I will tell it for you some day. Via del

C

Angelo Custode, is it, where you live? Good-day. You shall see me again;' and he walks off, leaving the children in such amazement that they almost forget Sandra's wonderful paper in the vague delight of the unknown man, who is to make Cesare a millionaire.

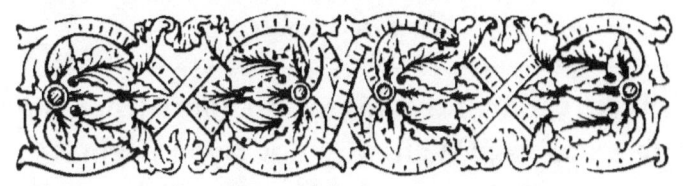

CHAPTER II.

THE MAGICIAN.

WHEN the children come home that evening, they find their father busily eating his supper of soup and yellow polenta—a kind of thick batter made with Indian corn-flour and water, which all the poor people live on in Italy—and their mother, Nita, chattering away after a very excited fashion. As she is a good deal given to talk at all times, the children are not particularly struck by this, and proceed to pull out their little earthenware basins and wooden spoons from a certain corner-cupboard, hungry as hounds for their supper.

'Well, Cesare, is that you?' says the mason, looking up from his plate. 'You are going to fall on your feet at last, I suppose?'

'Tell me, now,' chimes in Nita, taking the baby on her lap, 'what did he say to you? Yes, take some polenta, only go on talking all the same.'

The children begin to eat in silence, and Nita exclaims, 'Well, why don't you begin?'

'About what, mother?' says Bicè saucily; and gets a box on the ears for her pains, which causes her to subside into a corner and mingle tears with her polenta.

'Cesare, I am waiting to know what the man said to you.'

'The magician, do you mean, mother Nita? How could you tell? Were you there?' stammers Cesare, in confusion.

'All I know is that just before sunset a man came here and asked if a mason called Giuseppe and his wife Nita lived here, and had a boy called Cesare; and when I answered yes, he talked for a long while about all sorts of things I did not understand, and asked me whether I would let you go away with him over the seas to make your fortune. I do not understand how, but that is what he said, and he is coming to-morrow to hear the answer.'

'To go away with him?' repeats Cesare, bewildered. 'Would you send me away?'

'Not if thou art not willing, my boy,' says the good-natured mason, scraping up the last morsels of his polenta as he spoke.

'Now, Giuseppe, hold thy peace,' breaks in the shrill voice of his wife. 'Have we not enough to do to feed three mouths beside our own, without keeping also those who can get their living elsewhere? I have heard tell that the country of the English is rich and prosperous, and those who go there return with their pockets full of gold. Cesare shall go and win a fortune —eh, my son?'

Cesare grins, too much astonished to answer, and finishes his supper in silence; after which the three children climb a tiny rickety staircase to the garret where they sleep, under a broken roof and frameless window.

'O Cesare, I wish I were you,' whispers Nanna; 'to be going away into new countries, seeing all sorts of wonders, and getting plenty of money. I wish I were going too.'

'I wish you were, indeed; I do not like going so far away all by myself.'

'But you will make your fortune?' says Bicè, sitting upright in her little bed, with glistening eyes. 'O, I have heard so much of that place where the English live. Lucia says that the streets are all paved with gold, and every one rides about in carriages, and they eat off silver plates and wear silks and velvets all day long.'

'Just like the sermon we heard last Advent on paradise,' chimes in Nanna. 'Why, Cesare, it will be like going to heaven!'

'Only I cannot think why they want *me*,' muses Cesare doubtfully.

'Perhaps, dear Cesare, it is because the good God loves you better than us. He always loves orphans best, you know. Padre Giovanni said so.'

'I wish then that He would love you and take you too, Nanna mia.'

'O, I shall come some day, perhaps. If you get money very fast, you will be able to send me a letter with some gold pieces in it, and then I will come to you.'

'O yes, that will be very nice,' says the boy, brightening up.

'And send for me too. I am quite tired of sitting on the steps waiting to be painted. I'll tell you what we will do, Nanna: to-morrow we will all go and sell violets, and then find out the magician, the one that sells *buoni fortuni*, I mean, and get our fortunes told; and then we shall know exactly what will happen to us.'

'Yes, that will be just the thing,' they assent; and then they settle down to sleep.

But Cesare was too much excited even to shut his eyes for a long time. He thought over all his little life, beginning from the time mother Nita had told him of, when the big mason Giuseppe brought him home, a tiny brown baby wrapped in an old piece of flannel, taken from his dead mother's arms, when they found her lying cold and stiff in a dark corner of the streets at daybreak. Giuseppe had said, 'Let me take the boy, and he shall be as my own ;' and his wife Nita had scolded and grumbled a little at first, and ended by laying him in the rough wooden cradle, side by side with baby Nanna, and laughed and called them the little *sposi*, or betrothed ones. Since then he had grown up as one of them, running barefoot in the streets to beg a copper here and there, or help Nanna carry the baby out into the bright sunshine, and sit for hours on some bit of ruined wall, basking like a lizard in the sun.

Bicè, who is a year younger than Nanna and Cesare, is the beauty of the family and her mother's darling, and to her adornment goes every stray farthing which Nita can scrape together. Not merely for vanity, either, does she clasp red beads round the child's throat and hang long gilt earrings in her small ears; for many a 'foreign' artist asks leave to paint the pretty baby-like round face, with its solemn black eyes and rosy pouting mouth; and more than one silver piece had found its way to Nita's pocket in consequence.

Next day the three children set off earlier than usual to pick the freshest violets in the Borghese gardens, and sell them in the piazza; but, alas, Fortune favours them not, and even after they have managed to gain a few soldi they hunt in vain for the wonderful fortune-teller of the day before. Nita has charged them to be back before sunset, at which time the mysterious stranger promised to call again; so with weary and dispirited steps they make their way home.

'Well, have you thought over my proposal?' inquires the shabby man, taking the seat which Nita offers him, after carefully dusting it with her apron.

'Yes, signor; and we are very willing to let the child go.'

'And are you willing to come with me, little

one?' he asks of Cesare, who murmurs a somewhat doubtful 'Yes.'

'Well, you must just sign this paper, my good woman, to show that you give up the child willingly to me. I engage, you see, to feed and clothe him and take him as my apprentice for five years, during which time all his earnings belong to me. After that, he will be at liberty to earn for himself, or return home if he prefers it.'

'And may I ask, sir, what it is that you intend to do with him?' asks Nita timidly.

'Why, teach him to earn his living, to be sure. What, have you not heard of that wonderful England, where every house is a palace, and the streets shine with gold? O, he will make his fortune, I promise you!'

'Well, well, let us see the paper,' says Nita uneasily. She has a half-growing consciousness that were the child her own she would not let him go, yet now it is too late to draw back.

'You must sign your name here, if you please;' and he points to the place.

Nita takes the pen he offers in her clumsy fingers, and scrawls a big cross over the blank space.

'You cannot write, eh?' he remarks, in a tone

of satisfaction. 'Nor the boy either, I suppose?'

'Why, no,' she answers reluctantly. 'We were just thinking of sending him to the Christian Brothers' school. But no doubt you, sir, will teach him that and all manner of fine things.'

'O ay, I'll teach him!' he responds, with a sort of half-savage laugh, which sends a thrill of fear through poor little Cesare. 'And mind, he must be ready for me to-morrow morning when I call. We start early.'

'He shall be ready, signor.' And the door shuts behind him.

'O Cesare, it is very soon to go!' whispers Nanna, creeping close to him.

The boy's lips quiver, and his eyes fill with tears. He dare not say how repugnant is the very thought of going with that dark, scowling, cruel-faced man, for he knows that Nita grudges him his daily bread; and, child as he is, he longs to earn for himself and hear no more reproaches while eating the bread of charity.

Nita bustles about, gathering together his few poor clothes, and a lump of stale bread for his journey; and she tells the children to go up to bed and not talk all night, in a surly voice, dealing out meanwhile a double portion of polenta to Cesare for his last supper amongst them.

The children lie down without speaking on their little beds. Bicè cries herself to sleep, and Nanna turns her face to the wall silently.

Then, after a long silence, a little voice whispers,

'Are you asleep, Nanna?'

'No.'

'Will you think of me sometimes when I am gone, dear Nanna?'

'O yes; so often, until you come again.'

'Nanna, if I come back a rich man, will you marry me?'

'Yes, dear; indeed I will.'

'Give me a kiss, then.'

'There. Good-night, Cesare mio.'

And they lie down again, and sleep comes to them both till morning dawns.

Signor Giacomo, or 'Mr. Jack' as we should call it, makes his appearance very punctually next morning, and, without entering the house, calls to Cesare to 'come along.' The boy disentangles himself from Bicè's last embraces, and hurriedly presents himself before his new master, who bids him follow, and starts off down the stairs at a rapid pace. Nanna runs by Cesare's side, saying she will accompany him as far as they go on foot.

'What is that child doing there?' growls Giacomo, when he catches sight of her.

'I'm going a little way with poor Cesare,' she says, timidly looking up in his face.

'You'll do nothing of the kind, I can tell you,' he answers fiercely. 'Come, go back, or I'll let you taste my stick!'

Nanna's eyes flash; but she has wit enough to know that she cannot brave him, and must therefore attempt by cunning what she cannot obtain openly; so she says 'Good-bye' quite cheerfully, and turns her back to return home. No sooner have they fairly set off again than she crosses to the other side of the road and follows at a little distance, stopping from time to time to watch them.

'They are going to the railway-station,' she says to herself, as they turn into a desolate waste of new and half-built houses. And so they are. She watches them safe inside, and darts into the building, just in time to give Cesare a farewell hug while his master is absorbed in scuffling for tickets in the crowd. She watches from outside the loaded train pass screaming out of sight, and strains her eyes long for another glimpse ere she turns slowly homeward. And Cesare is gone, really gone! She must sell her violets alone to-day, and for many and many a long day afterwards, ere she and her little foster-brother meet again.

CHAPTER III.

ON THE BLUE SEA.

It is five days later, and Cesare is well on his way towards England. They have been from Rome to Leghorn by train, and there picked up three more little boys not much older than Cesare ; and now all four are lying, sick, lonely, and miserable, on the wet deck of a sailing vessel bound for London. Giacomo comes to them sometimes with an allowance of bread or soup, and tells them gruffly to get up and eat ; but otherwise he leaves them alone, to get over their troubles as best they may, only telling them that they had best try and find their sea-legs, as they will be a good three weeks on board that vessel, and he expects they will get pretty tired of lying upon wet boards.

Cesare is much strengthened in his belief as to England being heaven by the agonies of sea-sickness which he has undergone, and his first remark to one of his fellow-sufferers is to the effect that certainly this is purgatory itself; and therefore, since purgatory comes before heaven, the gate of paradise must be very near!

The boy to whom he makes this remark is a sturdy young peasant-lad fresh from the fields, whose ruddy face looks pale for the first time in his life, and who, cramped and wet through with the salt spray, looks ruefully out to sea over the ship's side.

'It must be a very good paradise, then, to make amends for *this*,' he murmurs, shivering as a great wave breaks over them.

'Have you come from far,' asks Cesare, looking up at his companion.

'From Tuscany,' he answers. 'And you?'

'I am a Roman,' returns the child, drawing himself up with a certain pride. 'I have never left home before.'

'Those two are Neapolitans,' the young peasant continues, nodding towards the sleeping pair. 'There are no Livournese, you see. They know better. They live always by the sea, and watch the ships going out, laden with boys like us, who do not know where we go, or to what; and they see the sailors and talk with them, and learn the secrets of that place over there.' And he points to the horizon.

'Do you think, then, that we are going to a bad place?' questions Cesare anxiously.

'I do not suppose that it is a very good one. Not quite paradise.'

'Why did you come, then?'

'Because I knew no more than you do. I was discontented at home and longed to see the world. Then this Giacomo came, as I was tending the vines, and he said, " Come with me and earn gold." And I came. Then he left me at Livourno and went down south to get you and the others, and I was kept shut up in a little wine-shop on the quay. I could not get away, but I saw and heard a great deal, and now I am afraid. However, we will not talk about it. Things may not be so bad as they say.'

'That is poor comfort,' sighs Cesare ; and he pulls himself up to a wooden bench at the side, and looks over at the blue water. The waves are rolling on, far, far as he can see, breaking into white crests of foam here and there, and now and then dashing against the bulwarks. He throws a bit of paper over the side, and watches it rise and fall and float out of sight, and then he tosses out a few crumbs from his last bit of bread, to see if the fishes will come and eat it. By and by one of the Neapolitan lads climbs up by his side.

'Well, what do you think of the sea?' he asks. 'I suppose you have never seen it before?'

'It is very wonderful,' says Cesare. 'Where does all this water come from, I wonder? I did not think there was as much in all the world!'

Mario laughs.

'This is an ugly sea, not like our beautiful clear blue water at Naples. You should see our bay, with its clear blue-green water, and all the fishing-boats going out, their large white sails dipping down into it, and great nets to catch the fish in hanging over the sides. And then the brown rocks and caves along the shore. One can look down into the water, O, so far, and see tall trees and sea-flowers underneath, with strange creatures walking or swimming about. And I can swim too. Can you?'

Cesare shakes his head.

'I never even *saw* water enough to get into, except our river, and that is so muddy and dirty one could not wash in it.'

'I hope there will be sea where we are going,'

breaks out Ceccho, after a pause. 'I don't think we could live without the sea.'

'That is because you are so accustomed to it. *I* don't want to see anything more of this horrible moving water. It makes me feel sick and miserable; but I am afraid there *will* be sea, for Giacomo said we should go all the way in this boat.'

'Tell us what your home was like, and why you left it,' says Ceccho, curling himself in a comfortable corner, and putting Cesare down beside him. And Cesare, nothing loth, tells all about Giovanni and Nita, Nanna and Bicè, and their home in the Via dell Angele Custode; and then the other in his turn begins a long story of his own and his little companion's homes. How they lived side by side in two houses on the borders of the sea; and 'Tonio had a father and brothers and sisters and a cruel stepmother, who beat him till he ran away, and said he would go anywhere to be free; and he, Ceccho, lived with his widowed mother, who was very poor, and when Giacomo came to them and told of the riches they might gain, he said farewell to the mother, and made his little bundle and came gladly, dreaming of all the money he would soon be sending her, and how he had promised to come back when his seven years' apprenticeship was over, that they might live happily together. So the boys talk and dream, and grow fast friends, and day by day the breezes blow upon them and bring the colour to their cheeks and joy to their hearts, as with the thoughtlessness of children they count the days which must still pass before they reach the golden El Dorado, London.

Giacomo is not at all unkind to them yet, perhaps because the boat is manned by Italian sailors, who would carry home tales and frighten other boys were they to see these roughly treated ; so beyond an occasional harsh word or cuff they cannot complain of ill-usage, and he serves out plentiful supplies of black bread or hard ship's biscuit, which is hungrily and thankfully despatched with appetites sharpened by the sea-air. Luigi is not as gay as the others. His heavy yet shrewd Tuscan brain is ever at work, under the uneasy suspicion that he has been 'taken in;' and he fears, with gloomy anger against himself, that perhaps after all it would have been better to stay amongst his father's vines and cornfields, and follow the plough over pleasant Tuscan fields, in a land where he knew and was known, than to have broken loose only to be ground down under the heel of a stranger, and toil for his daily bread in a foreign country. He is older than the others, too, probably about thirteen; while the united ages of the two young fisher-boys do not amount to much more than seventeen summers. And so he does not always join the play and chat of his companions, but sits alone, looking out to sea with a restless wild look in his eyes like that of a caged panther, wondering whether the horrible mistake he has made can ever be remedied, and how he can compass a return, or whether he had not best jump right off this plank into the foaming water beneath, and make an end of it all for ever. But then he has not been accustomed to water like those others who are laughing behind him, and pretending to catch fish with a bit of string; and he shudders at the thought of the cold waves closing round him and over him, and says to himself, 'No, I will wait.'

CHAPTER IV.

THE DESTINED HAVEN.

ALL things come to an end at last, and so does this voyage. One day, as the boys stand, as usual, grouped together, in the forepart of the ship, watching the pretty white-crested waves tumbling one over another, as the ship's bow cuts swiftly through them, a sailor up in the rigging shouts 'Land!' and his cry is repeated by others below. From this moment four pairs of eager eyes are constantly fixed upon the horizon, in the direction in which, as one of the sailors informs them, lies England. The excitable young blood thrills as a long gray coast-line is pointed out to them on the horizon, and who cannot guess the whispered comments which pass from one to the other as, hour by hour, new cliffs and headlands shape themselves out of the distance? And now they see houses; yes, and they are sure they can make out green meadows and forests of trees; and how they wish the captain would go a little closer to the land! Only, why is the sea so gray, the sky so leaden? Surely in this golden paradise the sun never ceases to shine?

Night closes in all too fast for their eager curiosity, and they are compelled to descend once more into the dark and dirty little hole, called by courtesy a cabin, where so many nights have been spent.

'The last night we shall pass on board!' exclaims Ceccho, as he tumbles into his berth. 'I wonder where we shall be to-morrow night?'

Luigi groans forebodingly of evil.

'Now, raven, don't croak,' laughs little 'Tonio; 'who knows what luck we may not get?'

'Let us keep together at all events, if we can manage it,' murmurs Cesare from his corner.

Ceccho's face falls at this suggestion. 'You surely do not think that he will separate us?'

'He will do pretty much as he likes, I fancy,' observes Luigi; 'we are just as much his *slaves* as any of the black people that old sailor was telling us about. Why, we cannot even make ourselves understood in any language but our own.'

'O, I shall try and learn English as fast as I can,' says Cesare, in a determined manner.

'Now do go to sleep, or to-morrow will never come.'

Next morning they are up with daybreak, and soon on deck, where a most novel sight awaits them. They are in the river, being towed along by a brisk-looking little steamer, past low dingy-looking coal-wharves and forests of masts, with houses looming gray and weird through the fog on either side. The smoke and raw damp mist make little 'Tonio cough, and all four stand in silent dismay.

'Dio mio!' exclaims Luigi at length, 'but this is worse even than I xpected!'

No one finds courage to contradict him, and he goes on: 'If *this* is England, may the holy saints see us well out of it! Not all the gold it contains will make me stay here.'

The other boys make silent observations as to dirt and misery too plainly seen, as they pass up and up, through crowds of shipping, and at length make preparations for landing. Giacomo now comes to look after his live cargo, and there is a tremendous amount of shouting and hauling and bustling, before they find themselves standing on dry land, surrounded with bales and packages of all descriptions, and Giacomo is being greeted by a short stout man, even dirtier and more villanous-looking than himself.

'So, these are the lads,' he exclaims, turning to them. 'Here, Jack, you go through the Customs, while I take them home.'

'All right,' nods Giacomo, in his foreign-sounding English. And the boys are all four stuffed into a rickety cab, with the dirty Englishman, who rejoices in the name of Mr. Stubbs. They jolt along in silence for the best part of an hour, without any attempt at conversation; then the cab stops with a jerk, and Mr. Stubbs, getting out, invites the boys to do likewise. They are conveyed into one of the houses, and up innumerable stairs too filthy for description, by a slatternly woman wrapped in a ragged shawl, and evidently the worse for liquor, and Mr. Stubbs presently joins them, carrying a big loaf of bread.

'Are you hungry?' he asks in bad Italian. They assent, and are presented with a hunch of bread each, while he goes on to inform them that for to-day they are free to amuse themselves; work will begin to-morrow. Now at last they are to know their fate. What does 'work' mean?

They do not venture down-stairs, but sit

huddled together at the window, looking down on the dirty street below, from which harsh voices and loud noises rise unceasingly. The sun comes out at midday, but only to draw foul odours from the gutters beneath and light up more recesses where dirt and misery strive in vain to hide. Ragged children fight and scream on the footpath, costermongers cry their wares, women throw stale food and refuse into the street, and chatter and laugh from their doorsteps, many with Italian face and voice, scolding at a tribe of black-eyed children in the Roman tongue. Such a strange medley of foreign elements! They catch a word here and there, and lean eagerly out of the window to hear the familiar sounds, but no one heeds them or notices the forlorn little strangers in their prison-like house. And so the day goes by.

Towards evening, when dusk has quite fallen upon the street without, and the poor children, neglected and uncared for, have fallen asleep in a heap on the floor (Ceccho and 'Tonio with their arms about each other's necks, and Cesare sobbing in vain for Nanna until his hot eyelids closed for a time upon the world, and he forgot his grief in slumber), there is a tramp of feet upon the stairs, and the door opens, admitting Giacomo with three lads at his heels, ruddy sunburnt youths of from thirteen to fifteen years, who clatter in noisily and throw down their burdens with exclamations of fatigue and disgust.

'Now then, supper! Where's the supper?' shouts one, stumbling over Ceccho on the floor. 'Hullo, who's this?'

'Dat is de new boys,' explains Giacomo, and adds in Italian to one of the new-comers, 'Go and talk to them, Beppo.'

Beppo peers into the darkness inquisitively, pulling down a chattering monkey in scarlet jacket and military cap, which has lodged itself on his shoulders and holds valiantly on by his black curls.

'How many are there of you?' he laughs, looking down at the little group. 'Stand up, and let us have a look. Well, you *are* little ones! I say, Jack, you *have* got them small enough this time!'

Jack grins complacently.

'Come along to supper, and I will talk afterwards,' he returns, ladling the contents of a huge smoking pot into the dish before him; and no further invitation is needed to make the boys fall to with a will.

'What is this place called?' whispers one of the little strangers to Beppo.

'This particular part of London, if you mean that, is called Saffron-hill, Hatton-garden,' he answers, translating the name literally into their own tongue.

'A garden! We have seen no garden,' returns Cesare, in wonderment.

'This is all the "garden" you are ever likely to see then,' laughs the other. 'They say it was a real garden once; but, if so, it must have been a mighty long time ago.'

'Where's Stubbs?' inquired one of the English boys, looking up from his plate. 'I have not seen him since yesterday.'

'Gone to pick up some kind of a grinder for one of these fellows,' responds Jack. 'He was too wary to provide himself before he saw them, and so he has got to do it now, for we cannot afford to keep them idle.'

'O, well, if he cannot find one they can be sent out begging,' chimes in the other boy. 'I am sure that fellow's pathetic face would draw heaps of coppers,' pointing to Cesare with his knife.

'His face is a fortune, isn't it?' laughs Beppo, and he turns to inquire of Cesare, 'Where did you say you came from?'

'Roma,' answers the child proudly, lifting his dark eyes to the speaker's face.

'Well, did you ever beg in the streets there?'

'Sometimes; and I sold violets:' and the tears come into his eyes as he thinks of Nanna and her basket full of fresh dewy flowers, sitting by the fountain.

'Ah, to be sure! Why, Giacomo, do you hear? That would be a good idea. He might sell violets here, until he is big enough to carry an organ.'

'So he shall!' and Jack thumps decidedly on the table. 'You go off to market to-morrow and get him some flowers, and show him the way to set about selling them, until he can shift for himself.'

So this is to be his fate! To exchange the sunny streets of Rome, the pleasant companionship of his little foster-sisters, the long bright days of idleness in a place where even work is sweet and mere existence a delight, for London streets and English misery—poor, friendless, and alone.

The Destined Haven. 45

He is sent off with Beppo early next morning to Covent-garden Market, where a shilling is laid out in bunches of violets; and then Cesare is taught how out of every two bunches to make three penny ones, mixing the flowers judiciously with leaves and disposing every blossom to the best advantage.

'You can get snowdrops too and primroses another year,' explains his instructor; 'but it is rather late for them now, and besides they do not last as well as violets. Mind you freshen them up every now and then by giving them a dip into water, and cover them well from the dust.'

Cesare thinks to himself that it will be very uninteresting work without any of the excitement of bargaining and cheating to which he has been accustomed, and he wonders how he is to make his fortune by selling violets in the streets of London rather than in those of Rome.

'O, you will not always do this,' his companion explains, as they sort and tie their flowers. 'As soon as you are a little bigger, you may carry an organ with dancing dolls, like me, and earn lots of money. Why, when I first came from Italy, three years ago, my master promised me twelve francs a month, that is ten shillings in English money; and now this one, Jack, gives me five shillings a week. I earn more than that, too; only of course he gets the rest, and I pay for my own board. If you could save up and buy a monkey or some dancing dogs, or something of that sort, you might set up on your own account. I shall, as soon as my time is up with Jack.'

'O, I should like to have a monkey!' exclaims Cesare gleefully. 'I wonder how soon I can begin to save? How much did yours cost?'

'It's not mine—it's Jack's; and it cost a good bit—thirty-five shillings? I've been saving up for three years to get one. No, you practise organ-playing when you come home at night, so as to make the handle turn nice and smooth, and then you can take my place some day. You are very small, though, for that. I cannot think why Jack brought such small boys this time,' he adds meditatively to himself. 'Now then, come on and let us begin our rounds. You may come with me for a day or two until you know your way about, or you will be getting lost.'

They pass up and down several streeets, Beppo good-naturedly giving hints and instructions in the intervals of droning out 'The Bluebells of Scotland' and 'Not for Joe,' and he finds himself rewarded by showers of halfpence which the sad dark eyes of the weary-looking little stranger draw from many a kind-hearted old lady. 'I think after all it pays to take you with me,' Beppo says, laughing good-humouredly, as they sit down on a doorstep to rest.

'I wish I could speak English though,' returns Cesare sadly.

'O, you will soon learn. And meanwhile it has not a bad effect, your Italian words and innocent pitiful-looking little face.'

'Do tell me, Beppo, is Jack a very cruel master?'

'Not a bit. He'll keep you without your supper if you don't bring home enough money, and give you a good thrashing if he finds you out in any cheating: but he is not at all a bad man, and you may have a happy life enough if you only work well and take things easy. I tell you what *is* hard, though, especially for the children who sell flowers and cresses in the street. It is the winter time, and getting up at five o'clock in the cold dark morning to be in the market by half-past, standing barefooted at the frozen pumps to break the ice and wash the cresses in cold water. Haven't I seen plenty of children shivering round, blue and numb with cold, and going off hungry to tramp about with cresses for people's breakfast-tables. One of our little ones got his feet stuck in frozen water that had splashed out upon them, and when he pulled them up all the skin and some bits of flesh were left in the ice. But never mind that, there is still the summer before you. Come on now.'

CHAPTER V.

WHAT OLD SIMPOLE SAID.

ALL through the hot summer months Cesare sells flowers in the London streets. The two Neapolitans are passed on to another master and go to live in the next street; Luigi or 'Luggy,' as the English boys call him, though 'Lewis' would have been the proper equivalent for his foreign-sounding name in their tongue, tramps about with a barrel-organ all day long, and with good food and some pocket-money has become reconciled to his fate. Beppo, having served his time, now goes out on his own account with the monkey which he has bought from Jack, and devotes his spare time to its training in the performance of all sorts of wonderful tricks, wherein he is heartily aided by Cesare. He, poor little fellow, has patiently plodded out day after day with his basket of violets, or sprigs of wired roses for gentlemen's buttonholes, or any other flowers the markets afford, and sometimes a plant or two, 'all agrowing, all ablowing.' But he does not like this flower-selling, which is sneered at by the others as being 'girl's work,' and he has petitioned Jack, who is not a bad master after all, and only beats him when he is 'not quite himself,' to let him have a cage full of white mice to carry about and teach pretty tricks.

As he has been very good and never found out in any cheating or mischief, Jack thinks he will reward him; so one day—just as flowers are getting scarce, and purchasers also—about the middle of August, he comes home at supper-time with a small wooden cage under his arm containing two tiny white mice.

Cesare jumps for joy.

'O Giacomo, how good, how nice! Beppo, come and see! Look at their dear little pink eyes and long tails! What will they eat? How frightened they are! O, I shall begin to teach them some tricks this very evening!'

'That is jolly!' says Beppo, laughing good-naturedly. 'Look what Cesare has got, Luigi!'

'Mice, eh? I think *I* ought to have them,' returns Luigi crossly. 'I could make them dance on the top of my organ. Every one is tired of those stupid dolls.'

'You sha'n't have them, then,' answers Cesare. 'You don't deserve anything, I am sure; you are always cross when I get anything nice. I might have lent them to you sometimes, but I won't now. No, I won't!'

'Won't you, indeed, Master Cesare?' snarls Luigi, giving him a pinch. 'We shall see.'

Cesare replies by digging his nails into the flesh of his tormentor with one hand, while with the other he tugs a good handful of hair out of his head, which is responded to by a stinging box on the ear; and finally Jack is compelled to pull them apart with a cuff to each, desiring them to sit down quietly to supper.

That night the tiny strangers are safely stowed away close by Cesare's bed, and in the morning he goes forth very proudly to exhibit them. His success, however, is not what he expected it to be; and he finds that the pretty little creatures need some training before they will consent to do anything besides poking their little noses as far as possible into the hay, or covering themselves all up in a corner, and only peeping cautiously out when they are quite sure that nobody is looking on. So the boy takes his little cage home, and goes off to a man in the same street, who keeps white mice and piebald rats for sale, and who, he thinks, will tell him how to train them. He is a little old man with one leg and a pair of crutches, very withered and rosy-looking, like a well-preserved apple, who lives on the ground-floor, in a little room all hung round with cages. Canaries, larks, gold- and bullfinches, linnets, white mice, rats, guinea-pigs, and parroquets line the walls, and make the air resound with their various cries. Such a singing and screeching and squeaking as goes on all day long! And, O, such a smell from the various fourfooted animals! Cesare himself, an Italian in the first place, and an inhabitant of Hatton-garden in the second, and who therefore might with truth have described himself as being 'not very particular,' afterwards declared to Beppo that the stench 'fairly knocked him down!'

'Tame white mice?' repeats the little old man, looking up from some trays in which he is sorting birdseed; for he sells that too, as well as all sorts of green-stuff, groundsel, and chickweed, and bits of turf with shamrock- or cloverplants upon them, meant to cheat the poor skylarks into the belief that they were free on the green earth (for larks, you know, though they soar so high to sing, build their nests among the grass). 'Tame white mice? O yes, it is easy enough. In the first place, you must get them well accustomed to you. Keep on looking at them and talking to them, and don't let any one feed them but yourself. Then you should give them their meals always at regular times, so that they may get to know when to expect you and look out for you. Why, all my creatures know as well as possible when dinner-time comes, and they will sit and watch just like children, and seem so pleased to see me, and jump up and scratch at the bars as soon as ever I come near them. Of course you must never *leave* any food in their cage, or they will never get fond of you. Then when they have lost their shyness, just open the cage-door, and let them come on your hand and eat there. Then by and by they will begin to run up your fingers and along your arm, and play about, like. But as soon as they know you, you may do anything with them. When I used to go out, I just kept two or three in each pocket, and put my hand in and took them out when I wanted them. They never ran away. Only when it was very cold they used to creep in at my neck and hide down in my clothes for warmth.'

'And how must I feed them?'

'Well, you can give them a little sopped bread, or a bit of cheese, or, in fact, almost anything. Don't you know how mice nibble at everything in one's cupboard? Bread-and-milk is the most wholesome food; but they are fond of a change, just as we are.'

'Well, I'll try, and thank you, sir;' and the boy moves towards the door, lingering, as he passes, to look at a bright-yellow canary in full song.

'Ah, he's a beauty, isn't he?' nods the old man, looking up. 'Got a fine coat, too, hasn't he?' This with a very satisfied chuckle.

'Yes, indeed, sir; I never saw such a bright one.'

'Ah, I guess you never did,' responds its owner. 'I've just been touching it up a bit.'

'How do you mean, sir?'

'Why, painting it, child. Do you suppose that is its natural colour?'

Cesare opens his black eyes in great astonishment, never having heard of such a proceeding before.

'Ah, I guess you don't know all the tricks of the trade yet,' laughs his little old friend good-humouredly. 'Well, never you mind, my lad; and if ever you meet with any misfortune, such as to lose your mice, just come round to me, and I'll sell you something cheap. There's guinea-pigs, now: many boys take them round; but they're stupid little creatures, *I* think.'

'I should like something lively and clever,' says Cesare. 'Something that I could pet and train up to do all sorts of funny things—a monkey, you know, or something of that sort.'

'Well, just save up some money as fast as you can, and I'll tell you what I'll do. You shall come with me to Jamrack's; that is the great place where all the wild beasts and curious creatures come when they send them from foreign parts, and he sells them again to the menageries all about the country. I *have* heard tell that he supplies those great gardens—"Zoological," I think they call them. Anyhow, it is a wonderful place, and you shall see it with me some day, and perhaps buy something very extraordinary in the way of an animal yourself.'

'O, that would be nice!' says Cesare, with sparkling eyes. 'Only please don't wait until I have money, for I am afraid that will be a very long time.'

'You must wait till I want something myself, at all events; and I must get rid of some of these first. But do not be afraid; I won't forget you. And now you had best be off, or your master will scold. You can come and see me again another time.'

CHAPTER VI.

'POOR BOBBIE!'

CESARE is not slow in availing himself of this permission; and before many days have passed he has tamed his mice sufficiently to be able to carry them in triumph to old Simpole, and coax him into a chatty mood.

'Don't you think I have done very well with them, Mr. Simpole?' he asks, holding out one in each hand as he speaks. 'I've spent hours and hours over them, and Jack is quite pleased to see how I make them come when I call.'

'Yes, you are getting on nicely. I think they would be tame enough now to learn some tricks. You should teach them to fetch and carry, and hold bits of bread on their noses, like dogs, without eating, until you give the word of command; and then put little coats on them, and make them dance on their hindlegs with a stick between their paws. I've seen mice dance like that on the tight-rope.'

'Can you teach them all that without putting their eyes out or hurting them in any way?'

'O yes. I don't hold with such practices; I don't even blind my birds, though everybody did tell me it was the only thing to make them sing. I'm sure I am not a bit cruel to my creatures. Why, you can only teach them by kindness— just kindness and patience, that's what does it. Some ladies have got a dreadful idea that we ill-treat our birds, though. I remember once, when I was showing off a lot of canaries I had, that used to draw a little carriage, and fire off popguns, and lie down "dead," and all sorts of amusing tricks, two little girls came up to look (young ladies, I *should* say), and began crying out, "O look here!" and "O how pretty!" and hunting in their little pockets for pennies, and of course I was pleased enough, and made them show off all their best tricks, when up comes their governess and calls out "Come away this moment, children!" and as they walked off, I heard her saying how cruelly these poor little birds were treated to make them do all these things, how they were starved and tortured and their eyes poked out with red-hot knitting-needles. It was not a bit true, and I'd like to

have told her so. Not that I suppose the birds
like some of those new-fashioned cages the *ladies*
have, where they can't drink a drop of water
without hoisting it up by some kind of a pulley,
like a bucket at a well. That is much more
cruel, *I* think, than our performances.'

'Yes, I suppose so,' says Cesare listlessly,
feeling very ignorant on the subject of birds and
their sufferings.

'We must all work, you know,' went on the
old man, scrubbing at a dirty cage with a bit of
flannel—'birds and men and women and everybody. We've all got to earn our bread in the
sweat of our brow, so we must just make the
best of it.'

'I don't see that,' answers Cesare, putting
away his mice, and sitting down on a low box
by the old man's side. 'The gentlemen whom
we see riding out in the Park on such beautiful
horses, or going to the opera and the theatre
every night, *they* don't work. The ladies, driving
in their grand carriages, dressed in velvets and
laces (just as I used to think *I* should do), they
don't work. It is only people who have got no
money that have got to work, and can't do as
they like. And I think it is all very unfair.'

'Well, I don't know much about the rights and the wrongs of it, laddie. I ain't no "philosopher," and I can't tell how we all came to be so different. But I know very well that I've got to work and that you've got to work; and if we don't, we starve in the streets or go to the workhouse. So that's pretty plain, I think.'

'Yes, I know; but what I mean is, why have not we all got alike? Why are we poor and other people rich?'

'O, dear! I don't know. I take things as they are, and not as they might be; and you had best do the same, child. These questions are too deep for such little heads as yours. Do you suppose, now, that your little mouse there is a-wondering why you keep sticking it up on its hindlegs, where it was never meant to be, when its own poor little nature is to run along on all fours?'

'Well, I don't know. Perhaps it is; only it can't speak, and so we don't understand what it wants.'

'Well, I reckon God can understand what we've got to say, anyhow, and He will make us rich enough when we get up to His place; so don't you trouble your little head about it. Did

I ever tell you about my poor monkey, "Bobbie," that died last winter?'

'No; do please tell me, Mr. Simpole.'

'Let me see; I think I've got his jacket now.' And he pulls out of a drawer a dirty square of scarlet cloth with ragged fringes and trimmings. 'Look here: he was so fond of picking at these beads, poor little fellow, he has pulled most of them off, do you see?'

'How big was he?' asks Cesare, examining the jacket curiously.

'Well, not very large, but he was a clever creature, and so fond of me. I never kept him chained or caged. He had his little bed there, beside mine, and sat on the corner of the table at meals, just like a Christian. And he had such cunning ways! Many and many's the time I've given the cat a tit-bit of meat before him, just for the fun of seeing him take it away. He would go up to her quite affectionately, and put one arm round her neck as if he was kissing her, and then holding her quite tight he would open her mouth and pull out the bit of meat. He would do it to me too. Oftentimes I have known him come up to me and pull my jaws open with his hands, and look into my mouth to see if there was anything to eat there. He was very revengeful too, and never forgot to give a sly nip to any one who had offended him, when he caught them unawares. There was a little girl lodging up-stairs once, whom he didn't like, and one day in the summer she had got a leafful of strawberries that some one had given her in the street, and she was carrying them up-stairs to her mother, who lay ill in bed, for she was a good little thing, very. Well, master Bobbie saw her, and up he was on the balustrades in a minute, and on her shoulder. Of course she screamed and began running upstairs; but he just nipped hold of her ear with one hand and pinched it black and blue, and with the other he clawed hold of the strawberries, picked them up one by one and swallowed down, the last just as she got to her own door.'

'That was not very nice of him,' says Cesare indignantly.

'No, it wasn't; but then, you see, he was nice to me, and so I liked him. The neighbours could not bear the sight of him; they used to scream out whenever they saw him, " O, here is that nasty beast again !" In fact, I believe they poisoned him at last; for he died, poor creature, in great pain. I gave him an emetic, but it did him no good, and he just came and huddled down at my feet, and moaned and looked up in my face with his bright eyes full of tears, almost speaking, as if he was trying to say, "O, I feel so bad!" I took him up and wrapped him in flannel and held him on my knees; and he just made up a little face, as he used to thank me with when I had given him anything nice to eat, putting down his ears and opening his mouth. And then he shivered a little, and stretched, and died. I tell you, my lad, I felt as bad as if I had lost a child.'

'They must have been nasty cruel people to poison your poor Bobbie,' says Cesare, full of sympathy.

'O, he was troublesome, there is no doubt of that; and we have no right to worry other people with our pets, you know. I've learnt better now; one always must learn by experience how to avoid mistakes, and giving pain to oneself and trouble to others. But that is easier to say than to do. Now go home, there's a good lad, and carry off your cage. I want to get my supper.'

CHAPTER VII.

ONE SATURDAY AFTERNOON.

ONE cold autumnal day in late October, two little girls are standing at their schoolroom window, looking disconsolately out at the heavy falling rain which drives in great sheets against the pane. A bright fire is burning, and the table is strewn with books, paints, workboxes, and various subjects of youthful employment. A large wax doll lies face downwards on one of the chairs, while a pile of calicoes and bright ribbons and stuffs, a pair of scissors, and a copy of the *Dolls' Dressmaker* bear witness to the industry of its little owner; while another corner of the table is occupied by some pictures from the *Illustrated London News,* half coloured, across which a couple of dripping paint-brushes have been thrown, making great blotches of vermilion and green where they fell. The little girls are fair, healthy, pleasant-looking children of about nine and ten, dressed alike in dark-blue serges and holland aprons, their long curls fastened back with a bow of ribbon. The elder of the two is busily rubbing one corner of the window-pane and straining her eyes to see as far as possible into the street; while the younger is engaged in that favourite amusement of children, which consists in breathing on a pane of glass until it is covered with a thin mist, and then writing with the nails on it.

'There, Janet; I have done my name beautifully. Just look: "Agnes Mary Haydon." Is it not plain?'

'Yes,' responds the other shortly, and somewhat ungraciously. .'Well, I suppose she will not come after all.'

'No, of course not. How could any one go out in such weather, Janet?'

'Is it not horrid? So disappointing, just when we were to have had such a nice afternoon at the Portland Bazaar! What is the use of having a holiday when one can't enjoy it?'

'I think that mademoiselle ought to give us another holiday on a fine day, since we cannot enjoy this one. Fancy, having to wait until next Saturday, a whole week, before going to choose our birthday present for father?'

'Yes, indeed, it is very provoking. Well, what shall we do all this afternoon?'

'O, I don't know. I don't care to do anything.'

'Shall we dress up, or play at ghosts and frighten somebody? Or ask cook to let us help her to make the pudding?'

'O,' bursts out Janet, 'I wish—I wish I were a cook, and had always something to do!'

'I should not like it,' answers Nessie. 'I could not bear to be always in that hot kitchen.'

'It would be better than being out in the cold and rain though, like that little boy there,' she says, nodding towards a solitary figure advancing up the square. 'Why, Nessie, just look; I do believe it is *our* little boy—the one with mice, you know!'

'So it is,' assents her sister eagerly, jumping down from the chair on which she has been kneeling. 'Janet, do you think we might have him in here?'

'I don't know; let us ask mother.'

'*You* run, then, while I stop him.' So Janet flies up-stairs and into her mother's room.

'O mother dear, our Italian boy is at the

door. May we have him in to show his mice, and play with them for a little while?'

'Hush, Janet, what a noise you make! Do you not see that your father is asleep?' and Mrs. Richardson draws her outside the room, and shuts the door. 'Now, speak gently, and explain what you want.'

Janet does so, while her mother looks out of the passage-window upon the street, where Cesare is shivering in the rain.

'Well, you may take him in, and let him dry his clothes at the fire, and give him sixpence. But mind that he wipes his boots well upon the doormat, and do not leave him alone in the room, or he might steal something.'

Janet is half way down-stairs before her mother had finished speaking, and the two children fly to the front door, and beckon Cesare to them.

'Will you come in and show us your white mice?' says Agnes shyly.

'Yes, missy, very glad;' and he steps into the warm hall.

'Come this way,' Agnes goes on.

'And wipe your shoes,' adds Janet, as they lead him into their cosy schoolroom.

'Now come and warm yourself. What is your name?'

'Cesare, missy.'

'Well, Cesare, why do you go out in such wet weather?'

'Because I have got to earn my bread, missy.'

'But could you not go out in fine weather, and stay at home when it rains?'

'O no, missy,' says Cesare, laughing, and showing his white teeth. 'Every day I must bring my master some money, or I get no supper.'

'How dreadful!' exclaims Agnes; and Janet whispers,

'Do let us give him something to eat!'

'We have no cake left,' returns her sister; 'it was all eaten yesterday.'

'Then I must ask cook to give us something;' and away she goes into the kitchen.

'Cook, can you give us something for a poor boy to eat.'

'What sort of a boy, Miss Janet, and where is he?'

'In the schoolroom. Mother said we might have him in to show us his white mice. He says he will have no supper until he brings home some money, and I am sure he is very hungry.'

'Well, you must ask your mother if I may give him anything.'

'O, I don't want to disturb her again, and she would be sure to say yes. Just give me a piece of bread, there's a dear old cookie!'

'Well, miss, here is a good thick piece of bread and some scraps of cold meat. That I am sure he does not get every day.'

'Thanks!' and she flies off with her prize.

'There, little boy, now eat that directly.'

'Thank you, missy, you are very good. My poor little mice were so cold that I have put them into the warm fender. When they are warm they shall play for you.' And he attacks the plate of cold meat with hearty goodwill, the two children looking on well content.

When the mice and their owner have been well warmed and fed, the little girls beg Cesare to begin his performances, which he does, and Mimi and Bibi are made to stand up on their hindlegs grasping a tiny stick at the words, 'Present arms!' to lie down motionless and 'dead' at command, to offer a funny little pink skinny paw by way of salutation, and various other devices of like nature. After going through them again and again, Mrs. Richardson and mademoiselle are brought down, and the whole thing is repeated, with many commendations and warm admiration from every one. Even cook leaves her pots and stewpans for a few moments to look in at the 'little foreigner and his tricks,' and declares she 'never saw such a *rum* thing, sure-ly; and quite a godsend for the little ladies on a wet day like this, when they usually worrit everybody's life out for something to do.' The children think there never were such wonderful animals; and Cesare, emboldened by success, takes care to tell them that kindness, and not cruelty, brings his pets into such perfect training, in spite of the ugly and false stories, which so many people believe in, of tortures inflicted on show animals. Then Mrs. Richardson questions him kindly about his home and life, and promises to go and see him some day, and perhaps get him admission to some ragged or night school, where he may learn to read and write, and so be fit for something better by and by. Finally a shilling is slipped into hand, and he is bidden to go home now and come again another day. 'On a Saturday, please, our half-holiday; and if possible a rainy one, that we may not be out.' So he promises to bring his pets as soon as they have learnt some new tricks, and then goes off, pattering along the street bare-headed and bare-footed, but warmed and fed and much elated with his success.

CHAPTER VIII.

AN EMPTY CAGE.

SOME weeks pass after this without anything occurring to break the monotony of the round of daily life among our Italian boys. One morning in late November, Cesare, lying awake in his little bed earlier than usual, bethinks himself of the young ladies in Russell-square, and how he promised to return as soon as his mice should have learnt some new tricks. They have been more tame and intelligent than ever lately, and only yesterday Bibi, the smaller of the pair, stood up on her hindlegs to beg a bit of cheese while Cesare was eating his supper. He must go and show the young ladies this, he thinks; and pictures to himself their bright welcomes and childish glee. And to-day—yes, to-day is Saturday, the very day they told him to come.

He jumps out of bed and dresses hastily, tossing a heap of sacking which forms his bedding over the still-sleeping Beppo, who wakens

An Empty Cage.

with a growl, and a 'Let me alone, will you?'

Now for Bibi and Mimi. He uncovers the little cage, and opens the door, calling their names as he does so. No one comes. Perhaps they are asleep. He sees Mimi lying in the farthest corner with outstretched limbs, and touches him softly with his finger to wake him. Mimi does not wake, but feels very cold. Cesare grows frightened, and pulls him out quickly by his tail. Mimi is dead! The boy gives a cry of horror, and tosses aside the hay, under which, alas, poor little Bibi lies stiff and cold also.

He cries out with grief and rage. 'They are dead, they are cold! Some one has killed my mice! Beppo, wake up and see!'

Beppo is by his side in a moment. 'E vero, it is true!' he exclaims, taking up first one and then another. 'And what has killed them? No cat, no weasel has got in here. It is not cold; they were covered well up; and besides the snow has not come yet. Let me look at the cage. Did you give them anything to eat last night?'

'Why, you know they ate their supper with me on my knee,' says Cesare, sobbing.

'Yes, yes; but did you put anything into the cage for them to eat?'

'No; you know I never do.'

'Well, but think now,' proceeds Beppo, putting on his clothes. 'Was the cage quite clean when you put them to bed?'

'Yes; I had cleaned it out when I came home.'

'Then look here,' Beppo continues, going to the cage, and pulling out some bits of cheese. 'Your mice have been poisoned!'

'And Luigi has done it!' almost shouts Cesare, in his excitement. 'I know he has! He was always so spiteful about my poor little mice; and he said long ago that he would pay me out some day for refusing to lend them to him.'

'Ah, it is he! Wouldn't I give him a thrashing if I were Jack! Now he has gone off for the whole day, see if he hasn't.'

Beppo's surmise turns out to be true. Luigi has departed on his daily round earlier than usual, doubtless to avoid the first glow of anger amongst his companions. The other boys, on hearing the news, rush in to handle the poor little dead bodies, examine the cage, and suggest various punishments for the offender. Giacomo swears a good deal, but declines to provide Cesare with any more mice, and tells the boys not to make a row about it; the creatures are dead, and Cesare must go back to his violet-selling, or sweep a crossing.

'Go off now,' he says, 'and find some work. If that old Simpole chooses to sell you something cheap, I'll stop it out of your money.'

This is a bright idea, and the boy, taking his bit of dry bread in his hand, darts off to the little shop round the corner, carrying his dead mice in his pocket, and full of his grief. Alas for this unlucky day! When he gets there he finds the shop shut up, and the 'first-floor front' informs him out of the window that the old man has gone out selling green-stuff on a hand-barrow.

Cesare turns away in blank disappointment, and saunters down the street. Where shall he go? He looks up the little dark narrow archway leading to his church, the Italian's church, and thinks how many weeks it is since he went in there, or even said his prayers. Well, he will go in now and rest a bit in the quiet place; so he pushes the heavy door open, and steals quietly to a corner, and kneels down upon the pavement.

The service is going on, and he tries to remember what prayers he used to say in Rome; but he has almost forgotten them, and could not read even if he had a book; so he leans his head against a pillar, and watches the familiar sight of the priest at the altar. And by and by he finds himself saying words half aloud, in the sweet Roman tongue, 'Our Father.' It is the only thing he can remember, and he repeats it over and over, wondering if God really hears it, and whether He cares about poor Cesare and his sorrow. He takes the tiny stiffened bodies out of his pocket, and lays them on the pavement before him, wondering as he does so whether God could bring them to life again, and if it would be any use asking Him. He remembers hearing a story once, of how 'the good Jesus' raised a poor boy to life, and also a little girl. He had heard it in a sermon one day, when he and Nanna strayed together into a church during the Lenten season. But he does not think God cares about animals, or brings them to life again. Nita used to say it did not matter what happened to the beasts. She would kick and beat the cat, and laugh when her husband flogged his mule; and even gentle little Nanna did not mind, for she said, 'They have no souls, all those creatures.'

Cesare wonders what has come to him to make him so tender-hearted over a couple of mice. Only two white mice, and yet he had cried over them! Well, it must be because he had no one else to love that he had grown so fond of Mimi and Bibi. They were so clever too—so unlike any ordinary mice. He had spent all his time for months in teaching and training them, and now they were just perfect; and all his time and trouble were wasted! He would have to work for a whole winter before he got any other mice to do as well, and even then— Ah, he would never have the heart to do anything again! And he breaks out into fresh tears, and takes up his poor pets and holds them on his knees, clasping his hands over them, and looking up to the altar, with a whisper of, 'O God, *please* make them alive once more!' They do not stir, and he says 'Our Father' again slowly. No answer from the altar or movement in the little bodies, and he begins to think of all the scoffs and jeers he has heard against God's power, and how Jack never goes to church, and says it is no use, for no one hears; and Beppo thinks that if there is a God, He does not trouble about us down here. Perhaps what they say is true.

'If God does care about me, as Nanna said He did, He ought to punish Luigi for being so wicked and cruel. Ah, I *hate* Luigi! I wish I were strong, that I might beat him till he cried. I wish I could break his organ or poison his food, or do something that would hurt him very much. I wonder'—here a fresh thought comes to him, and he lifts his head again—' I wonder if God would punish Luigi if I asked Him? Perhaps He might put him into hell. I know where hell is; it is a great fire in the middle of the world underneath our feet. I have seen pictures of it in the churches at home. Great yellow and red flames, and horrible devils with long pitchforks, tossing the wicked souls into the fire. How Luigi would howl in there!' and the vivid Italian imagination lights up his eyes, as he tries to recall the old familiar paintings on church- and cloister-walls.

The service ends, and the building is empty again; but still Cesare dreams on, forgetting time and place, his untasted breakfast and the day's work before him, his cramped limbs chilled by the stone pavement, and his little head all confused with perplexity and grief.

By and by he is roused by a light touch from the half sleep into which he had fallen, and, looking round, he sees a little lady dressed in black, not very young or beautiful, but with a sweet smile and sad loving eyes, who is speaking to him in his native tongue.

CHAPTER IX.

THE FAIRY GODMOTHER.

CESARE was little aware of the picturesque attitude into which he had fallen, nor of the quiet little black-robed figure which has been watching him so attentively for some time past. He is half kneeling, half sitting, at the lower end of the church, leaning against a great stone pillar. His hastily-put-on jacket is open in front, showing the bare bronzed throat, over which a mass of tangled black curls fall in profusion, shading forehead and neck. His eyelids are heavy from crying, and at his side lie the two dead mice, a ragged cap, and a piece of bread, which had been given to him for his breakfast.

'What is the matter, poor little one?' says the soft voice in Italian.

'They are dead, my little mice! Luigi killed them,' says the child, holding up the bodies.

'Will you come outside the church? I want to talk to you,' says the strange lady; and as she moves towards the door, Cesare perceives that she is slightly deformed. She questions him kindly, about his life, home, and manner of living, and then says, 'Would you have time to come and see me this afternoon? Here is my address;' and she hands him a card.

'I cannot read,' says Cesare, shaking his head.

'Ah, that is true; I daresay not. Would you like to know how to read?'

The child flashes a bright look of assent.

'Well, perhaps I may teach you some day, if you are good. Meanwhile, let me see. You can go across Leather-lane, up Baldwin's-gardens, and a little way down Gray's-inn-lane, and then ask some one to show you Guildford-street. I live there, No. —. Come at three o'clock;' and she nods good-bye and leaves him.

Cesare looks after her as she passes up the street, and wonders whether *she* is a *buona fortuna* come to him at last. She looks very unlike any ordinary woman. Very like a fairy godmother, or a witch, or something of that description. If Cesare had ever read the story of Cinderella, he would have looked out for pumpkins and mice soon after; but he does not know any such legends. The only ones he has ever heard are those of St. Dorothy with her roses, or St. Elizabeth with a lap full of loaves, or the quaint childlike St. Francis preaching to birds and fishes—none of which were at all like this lady. So he eats his bread on a doorstep, and wonders what he shall do with himself all day until three o'clock comes. It is too late now to buy flowers or cresses in the market, and he shrinks from going home. Old Simpole is out, and all his young companions going their rounds; so he wanders through the busy streets, holding out his grimy little hand to beg a halfpenny with which to get some dinner. Towards two o'clock he turns homewards, and as he walks along, a sudden thought strikes him. Shall he go and tell the young ladies in Russell-square of his misfortune? No sooner has the thought occurred to him than off he starts at a run, and is in a short time standing at the door panting and breathless. He had almost expected to see their faces at the window, watching for him; but no, they are not there.

'They are gone out,' calls up cook from the kitchen-window; 'so you be off!' and she shuts down the window with a bang.

Another disappointment. Cesare almost

cries at the thought. He walks slowly away, and leans against the bars of the square garden-railing watching a group of merry children playing at Puss-in-the-corner. Presently, to his great joy, he catches sight of little Miss Janet amongst them.

'Missy, missy!' he calls, pushing his hands through the bars and waving them to attract her attention.

'O, there's Cesare and the mice!' she cries, and runs up to him, all the children following.

Cesare pours forth his tale of sorrow, the little crowds of children listening attentively and sympathisingly.

'O dear, I'm so sorry!' says Janet when the tale is finished. 'And what are you going to do with them?'

'I don't know, missy. I never thought about it.'

'Let us make a funeral and bury them in our garden!' exclaims Nessie.

'Yes, do,' chimes in another; 'it will be such fun.'

Cesare looks from one to the other somewhat ruefully.

'Would you like them to be buried nicely in

our yard?' inquires Janet, in a patronising tone. 'You might come and see their grave sometimes, you know; and we will plant it with flowers, and make it quite pretty.'

'Thank you, missy.'

But poor Cesare is too subdued by his misfortunes to smile, when the little girl proceeds to lead the way into their house, and darting up-stairs, presently returns with a small wooden cigar-box, some bits of crape, and five dolls of various sizes.

'I am going to put all my dolls into mourning,' she says, twisting a bit of crape round Cesare's cap. 'Here is the coffin; put them in!'

The boy does so, and all the children stream after him into the yard, where, in the very midst of the children's flower-bed, a grave is dug and the box deposited therein. When it has been duly filled in, the children scatter flowers over it, and begin a lengthy discussion as to what plants they would buy to make it bright; in the midst of which Cesare suddenly remembers his appointment, and begs to know the time in great trepidation.

'Five minutes to three,' sings out the messenger who has been despatched indoors to inquire.

'O, I must go,' says Cesare, preparing to make his farewell bow.

'Where are you going?' they ask.

'To see a lady. Here is her name.'

And he pulls out the little card from his bosom. The children look at it and exclaim,

'Why, that is our aunt Jane!' And a multitude of questions ensue, which the boy can scarcely answer, so anxious is he to be gone.

'Well, come again soon!' they cry, as he touches his cap at the door. 'You will want to come now that we have got your grave!'

Miss Jane Haydon is sitting alone in her study, waiting for Cesare, and when he arrives she makes him sit down and rest, and eat a piece of bread-and-butter before she begins to talk. It is a good-sized room, at the top of the house, with carpetless floor and little furniture. A large easel stands near the window, and two or three seats are grouped here and there, while on the sofa a ghastly lay figure is stretched, with rosy face and skeleton arms, clothed in a Roman toga. A long wisp of fair hair hangs over the easel, which makes Cesare shudder. Is this strange lady a witch, and has she decoyed him here, to kill, and perhaps eat, him, and afterwards hang his scalp by the side of that fair tress? But she is the aunt of his two dear young ladies, so after all she cannot be so very bad, and he looks round with more confidence upon the walls lined with pictures (framed and unframed), sketches, unfinished portraits, and prints. Presently she speaks.

'I want you to sit to me for your portrait, my boy. I think that your face would just do for a picture I am at work upon; and if you can come to me every day, in the morning, I will pay you fourpence an hour.'

Cesare's heart leaps with delight, and he gladly undertakes to come at any hour and for as long as the lady wishes.

'Very well, then, we will begin on Monday next, at eleven o'clock. Mind you are punctual.'

'O yes, signora; indeed I will be here in good time: but—' he hesitates and looks down, 'I am afraid I have no other clothes than these.'

'I should hope not, indeed,' returns the lady sharply. 'At least, I would not have you in any others. Why, it is just those rags which are so artistic! But you do not understand anything about that, of course. How should you? And it is better not.' She goes on talking to herself, forgetful of Cesare's presence. 'By the bye, I saw you in church to-day: do you go often?'

'No, signora, I have not been for a long time. Only I was in trouble, and I wanted to ask God something.'

'What were you saying?' questions the lady, laying down her brush and looking curiously at him.

'I asked Him to bring my poor little mice back to life again, and He did not,' answers the boy mournfully.

'Perhaps God *has* answered your prayer—and mine, after all—only in another way,' she whispers softly. 'Go again to-morrow, my boy.'

'I will, signora.'

CHAPTER X.

A LONG TALK.

CHILDHOOD'S sorrows are soon forgotten; and so much has happened on this eventful day that Cesare comes home quite bright and merry, though without a farthing in his pocket, and chats out his adventures gaily enough. The little empty cage, indeed, gives him a pang as he catches sight of it, but he pretends not to care when Luigi maliciously inquires after them. 'I know you killed them,' says the child quite steadily, fixing his eyes upon his enemy, 'and I am too small to thrash you for it. But I will never forgive you.'

Luigi turns away with a laugh, and though his companions show their displeasure by 'sending him to Coventry' for a day or two, the affair is soon forgotten. Old Simpole is so sorry for the boy that he gives him two more white mice, and exhorts him to keep a good heart and begin all over again; and he goes every day to Miss

Haydon's studio, bringing home each time a bright silver sixpence, part of which Jack allows him to keep for himself. Those afternoons are the brightest spot in Cesare's life, and he grows merry and happy as in the old days, when he and Nanna ran bare-footed along the Roman streets, pelting each other with withered violets or fountain-spray under the fierce burning of the Southern sun.

'Well, little one,' says his kind friend, smiling as she lifts her head from the canvas on which she has been silently at work for an hour or more, ' are you very tired ?'

'No, signora, indeed ; but what if I were ? It would be a pleasure to be tired in your service.'

'Little Italian,' she laughs, ' you are a true child of the South. You cannot even answer one plain question without a compliment.'

'O, it is not a compliment at all, signora ; it is the truth. You are so good to me, and I can do nothing for you.'

'I assure you, Cesare, you are most useful to me, as well as a great pleasure,' returns the lady. 'There now ; I can make pretty speeches as well as you. Well, it is getting too dark for painting,' she continues, laying down her brush, 'so come closer to the window and take your lesson.'

Cesare closes the accordion, which he has been holding extended, with a long wail of discordant notes; slips it into the case, and pushing his stool to the window, begins to read, in a high-pitched voice, 'A cat was in a bag;' and so on for some time. Presently he lays down his book with a preoccupied air, and looking up in Miss Haydon's face, says, ' Signora, why are some people rich and some poor? Why cannot we all be alike?'

'What has put that into your head, little one?' she answers, looking half amused, half vexed at his question.

'I have thought about it for a long time. Never at home (in Italy, I mean), because there it is not so hard to be poor. One has always the bright sun and the pleasant air, and polenta to eat, and beautiful things to see. No one wants to be rich there, except, perhaps, children like Bicè, who long for fine dresses and pearls. But *here* it is all so dull and heavy and cold and miserable, I cannot help longing to drive about in a fine carriage and be rich and get a little leasure, and not do any work.'

'Ah, not do any work! How would you manage that, Cesare mio? All those fine ladies and gentlemen have their work to do, just as well as you and I have. Whether they *do* it or not is another question, but certain it is that they have it to do.'

'Not such hard work as ours, then,' murmured the boy, looking down and making dogs' ears of the leaves of his spelling-book.

'Yes, harder sometimes. Hard in a way you could not understand, Cesare. It is so difficult to explain,' she goes on, talking to herself; 'how can *they* understand *our* work? For instance,' she turns to Cesare again, 'look at *my* work. Any of you boys who have to go out in all weathers, wet or fine, sometimes without a crust to eat, or with the fear of being beaten when you get home, might look at me and think, "Dear me, I wish I had that lady's work to do! How very easy it must be to sit indoors all day in a cosy warm room, and paint pretty pictures in bright colours! I should not mind having *that* work to do." Come now, have you not sometimes had this thought yourself?'

'Yes,' says Cesare, smiling and colouring.

'And you did not know, did you, of the long,

long years of learning that went before, when I drew "strokes" or "rounds" all day long. How I worked and studied at the drawing-school as a young girl, when the bright days passed by, from morning till night, and I sat at my easel longing and longing to be out in the free air and sunshine. Or how, even now, I look out of window sometimes on a fine day, and think how nice it would be if I could send for my carriage and take a long drive right out into the country, or even go for a little walk in the square. Instead of which I have to finish my picture, and paint on and on until my back aches and my head grows tired and my eyes can scarcely see. Believe me, my boy,' she goes on after a pause, 'every one in this world has his appointed work, only we do not always know what other people's work is, nor how hard. I know as little about the work of a countess at court as *you* knew about mine until now. It is no concern of ours what other people do of their work, and the lower cannot always comprehend the higher; but it is of great importance that we should both *know* and *do* our own.'

'Then, signora, I suppose my work is earning money for Jack?'

'Yes. And it is not *very* unpleasant work to come and sit as my model, is it?' she adds, smiling. 'I know some one who would not be sorry to change places with you.'

'O, who, signora?'

'Well, when I went to see my little nieces the other day, I found them in great tribulation over a slateful of sums which they had to prepare for their lessons next day, and one of them said very much the same thing as you have just been saying. "O dear auntie, I do think it is very unfair that we should have so many lessons to learn. We are always doing lessons, lessons, lessons, and what is the use of it? I wish I was a little boy in the strects who didn't know how to read and write and had not got to learn! I wish I was Cesare, who has only got to walk about and play with his mice all day, and never have any horrid sums or French or music to do!"'

'And what did you say?' asks Cesare astonished.

'Very much the same thing that I have been saying to you. "Whatsoever thy hand findeth to do, do it with thy might." God will ask us all one day what we have done with the talent that He gave us. You remember the story I told you the other day of the " Talents" ? Well, we shall have to answer to God for the use we have made of everything we possess.'

'What is *my* talent, signora ?'

'You have a talent of *health*, which enables you to walk about for hours untired, earning money. Then you have a *mind*, which can learn and remember and invent and pick up all sorts of knowledge. You are using one talent by carrying about mice, to earn pennies by showing them ; and another by learning to read. I could tell you much more were it not growing late ; but now I am going to ring for tea, and you may stay and have some too. See here ; I will give you twopence, and you can go to the nearest baker's shop and buy two muffins, one for me and one for you, and then come back and toast them !'

Cesare's face beams with delight, and he departs on his errand. When he returns, the kettle is singing on the hob, a white cloth spread over the table, with tea-tray, bread-and-butter, and Miss Haydon's armchair drawn up between it and the fire, while Cesare's little stool occupies the opposite corner. The muffins are toasted and eaten, and several slices of bread-and-butter after them, while Miss Haydon lies back, tired, in her chair.

'Will you pour me out another cup of tea, my boy?' she says. And Cesare proudly and delightedly fills her cup, very carefully dropping in a lump of sugar and handing it to her.

'That's right. I wish I had some one always to wait upon me. I am rather lonely sometimes.'

'Are you, dear signora?' whispers Cesare, in wistful surprise.

He had never dreamed that his sweet bright instructress could possibly be otherwise than perfectly content, having had little experience as yet of other than bodily wants. She rouses herself presently to talk and amuse the child.

'What a pretty picture that one is!' he remarks, pointing to a large oil-painting which hangs over the mantelpiece. It represents an open doorway, with sprays of convolvulus climbing up the side, clothing the whole bare wall with brilliant colouring. On the step a child of about three years old is sitting, dressed 'in a white-cotton frock and little black shoes, through the holes in which her red socks are peeping. She is evidently engaged on her first piece of patchwork, and bends over it with intent and flushed face; while in the background another girl, some years older, holds up a rose which she has just cut with the pair of scissors in her other hand.

'Those were two little girls I saw in the street one day,' explains the artist; 'and I asked them to come and sit to me, and found out all about them. That pretty fair child in front is "Annie," an only child, and the pet of her father and mother, who are poor but respectable people living near here. The other one, with dark eyes and a thin white face, has a very unhappy home. Her father is a drunkard, and beats and ill-uses poor little Esther and her brother. Their mother is dead.'

'Where are they now?' questions Cesare, his eyes fixed on the picture.

'Esther is at home, at least in the wretched garret they call "home," beaten black and blue by her father almost daily. And little Annie, whom every one loved and cherished, is dead.'

'I am so sorry; I should like to have seen her,' whispers the boy to himself.

'She died of scarlet fever,' goes on Miss Haydon. 'I often went to see her during the three weeks of her illness, and they did not seem to apprehend danger, though her mind wandered continually. She lay quite quietly on her little bed talking to herself, counting the flowers of the paper on the wall, and calling to her little companions by name. Sometimes she seemed answering some one who was asking her to do something wrong, for she repeated over and over, " No, no; that would be naughty ; I must not do it! *She* would not like it" (I think she meant me), "and God would be angry." They sent for me when she grew worse; and she knew me then, and turned her little face towards me with a sweet smile, saying, "Good-bye!" and then she looked up in her mother's face and said, "Dear mother, I do love you. When I go to heaven, I shall ask God to send down an angel and fetch you too." And she shut her eyes and leaned her head on her mother's breast, and fell asleep, and when we looked she was dead.'

CHAPTER XI.

IS HE DEAD?

CESARE sits very still on his little stool for some time after this story, with his eyes fixed meditatively on the picture over the fireplace. Presently he breaks out again,

'Was she a very good little girl when she was alive?'

'Very good, my dear.'

'I am not at all good, signora. I should like to be good, that people might love me.'

'That is not a right reason,' says Miss Haydon gently; 'you must be good for the sake of pleasing God.'

'I do not think I can,' he answers, shaking his head; 'it is too hard. I should have to forgive Luigi.'

'Suppose,' says his instructress, fixing her eyes upon him gravely,—'suppose you were to die to-night, Cesare, would you be fit to go to God?'

'I don't know, signora.'

'Come nearer to me, little one;' and she lays her hand on his head, and talks softly to him for a long time, questioning, counselling, and answering in turn. By and by she rises and goes to the window.

'My boy, you really must go now. I have kept you too late. It is nearly nine o'clock, and there is a thick fog in the streets. Will you be able to find your way home?'

'O yes, thank you, signora.'

'Here is your money then; run away. Goodbye!'

'*A rivederla, signora!*' And he runs gaily down the stairs, turning back for one last look at the little black-robed, pale-faced, deformed woman who is his one friend in all the world.

The streets are dim and yellow with fog, and fewer passengers than usual are astir, as Cesare dances along, touching the railings of the houses from time to time to make sure of his position. Here and there a man waves a blazing torch at the corners of the streets, piloting some stray foot-passenger along a crossing, or a cabman shouts at intervals as he drives slowly past. The boy is absorbed in thought of all he has heard and seen to-day, and without stopping to listen for advancing wheels, he begins to cross the crowded thoroughfare.

Suddenly a plunge, a scuffle of horses, a shrill scream, and Cesare is lying under the wheels of a carriage, bleeding and insensible. Policemen hurry to the spot ; he is lifted gently up and laid upon the pavement.

'Well, you've done for the child, I believe !' shouts a policeman angrily to the cabdriver. 'What on earth made you go like that, without even giving a call, in this weather ?'

The driver lashes his horse and struggles to get away ; but the policeman holds the animal's bridle with a firm hand.

'Give up your address, come ; and where's your number ?' And he is obliged to produce both before they allow him to drive off, growling and swearing under his breath.

Meanwhile three or four policemen and a neighbouring chemist, surrounded by a small crowd of the description which so invariably accompanies a street-accident, have been trying to restore the poor boy to consciousness, but in vain.

'Is he dead ?' inquires the first policeman, bending down to look at him.

'Not quite; but I'm afraid he is dying,' answers the chemist's assistant, moistening the white lips with a few drops of brandy-and-water.

'We must send down to the hospital for a litter to take him in.'

'Ay; I'll go,' answers another, and sets off down the street in as quick a run as the yellow curtain of fog will permit. Meanwhile, the other men gently chafe the little lifeless hands, unfasten the clothing, and put some drops of brandy into his mouth.

'Did he swallow it?'

'No.'

'It is a very bad case, is it not?'

'I expect so.'

'Poor little chap! I wonder who he is. Perhaps he has a mother at home—looking out for him, maybe.'

'Wonder if he has got anything in his pocket which may serve to identify him?'

'O, they will find out all that at the hospital.'

'I suppose they are sure to take him in?'

'O, they can't refuse, at this time of night.'

'Can't they, though? I've seen plenty turned away.'

'Not from this one, I'm sure. It is a free

one, you know. You don't want orders of admission or tickets or anything. They just take in whoever is ill, as long as they have room for them. Why, only last week I helped to carry in a woman who was burnt, after midnight, and they were all up in a minute, as kind as possible.'

'Well, what a time they are coming! O, here they are! Here's the litter!'

The child is carefully lifted in, and the little procession tramps slowly down the street, and in at the great arched gateway. Across the courtyard, where a woman stands beckoning.

'In here, men's ward,' she whispers.

And they lay him on a bed, and nurse and surgeon together examine the little sufferer.

'Any bones broken, sir?'

He nods gravely.

'The wheels passed over here and here. Internal injuries too, I fear.'

So he is undressed and laid in the bed, and remedies applied; and by and by his dark eyes open wonderingly, and he looks round.

'Where am I?'

'Quite safe, my dear,' said a strange voice soothingly. 'Don't talk now, but go to sleep, and you will be all right in the morning.'

And the child's head droops on the pillow, the weary eyes close, and he sleeps.

Towards morning he awakes, in great pain; and then for some hours he has only a confused sense of faces and voices round him, the touch of gentle though firm fingers closing over the pain, and then utter unconsciousness. When he awakes it is night again, and the same kind nurse, who had received him into the ward at first, is nodding sleepily over the fire. He is in a long lofty whitewashed room, with rows of beds all down the walls on either side. He tries to count them, but cannot do it, his head feels so confused; and then he looks at the inmates, many of them asleep, some lying awake staring blankly before them, with patient upturned faces; and one man is groaning softly to himself.

Some of the beds have curious mounds in the middle, like hencoops under the bedclothes, and as he looks down at himself he finds that he has got one too. He turns his head feebly on one side to look for his little mice, and finds they are not there; and then he tries to speak, but his mouth is dry and parched and black with fever, so that no sound comes. Then he dozes again, and wakes to find a spoon held to his lips with something very soft and cool and refreshing in it. He is too weak to talk, however, and lies silently wondering what is the matter with him, and how he comes to be in this strange place.

By and by eight o'clock strikes; the day nurse comes in, bright and brisk after her night's rest, and his kind ministrant goes off to bed, while her successor pokes up the fire, sets on a big kettle to boil, and serves out tea to all the patients. Then, after putting away the tea-things, she goes round with basin and sponge to wash their faces and tidy them up for the day. Those who can bear it have their beds made, and some sit up to read or otherwise amuse themselves; one or two get up and dress, and try to help nurse in waiting upon their fellow-sufferers. Cesare watches it all with languid interest, and manages to smile a good-morning when his turn comes for the basin and towel.

'You are better to-day, are you not?' smiles the nurse, looking pitifully down upon the small white face.

'Yes, ma'am, thank you.'

'Are you glad to have your face washed again? Where are your little hands? Now for the hair! Why, what long black curls, almost like a girl's! You are a foreigner, are you not?'

'Yes, ma'am; I come from Rome.'

'Dear me, what a long way off! Have they got any nice places like this in Rome?'

'I don't know, ma'am; I never saw any.'

'Well, now you look quite smart. All ready for the doctors. They will be here in a minute, so I must make haste.' And away she bustles to the next bed.

The doctors come and examine Cesare, and talk a great deal, and finally smile at him and tell him he is getting on very well; and then they go on their round, many of the poor white faces brightening visibly at their approach, while each has some story to tell of 'such pain in this here leg,' or 'a very bad night,' or, more rarely, an acknowledgment that 'I'm a little better to-day, thank you, sir.'

'You'll be having your friends to come and see you very soon, I expect,' says nurse, sitting down by Cesare's bed that afternoon. 'To-morrow is visiting-day, when patients' friends can come and see them, so you may look out for visitors.'

'O, I don't think any one will come to see me,' sighs Cesare.

'Yes, they will,' nods nurse; 'there was some one inquiring about you this morning.'

'Was there? O, who?' Cesare almost jumps up with delight.

'A boy with a barrel-organ, I think. They told him to come to-morrow afternoon.'

'That's Beppo,' says the child, smiling to himself.

'Well, now try and take a little sleep, that you may be well to-morrow,' says nurse, tucking him smoothly in, and pouring out his medicine. And she leaves him to fall asleep and dream of Beppo, and little Annie and the doctors, all mixed up together in a strange nightmare of confusion.

CHAPTER XII.

VISITING-DAY AT THE HOSPITAL.

THE next day is Friday, and all the occupants of the long lines of beds make themselves extra tidy and clean, and hurry somewhat over the midday meal in their anxiety to be quite ready when two o'clock comes. Many and many a pale face is turned towards the door, and eager eyes watch for its first opening, longing for the sight of some familiar face.

The first to come in is a poor woman with a baby in her arms, and another clinging to her skirts. She passes down swiftly to the very end of the ward, where her husband is lying with a fractured thigh; and whispered greetings pass between them as she smooths the pillow tenderly under his head, and lifts the toddling child for a kiss. Then two men saunter in, and go up to the man nearest the door, whose head is swathed in bandages; then two or three more women; and presently a rough black head is thrust in at the doorway, and Beppo, peeping in, stares round with astonished gaze, his eyes wandering from one bed to another in search of his little friend.

Cesare feebly tries to call, and nurse, coming forward, leads Beppo to his side.

'Cesare, poor little Cesare, is that you?' he cries, in Italian; and he kisses him rapturously on both cheeks, in true foreign fashion.

'Dear Beppo, how good of you to come and see me!'

'How ill you look!' says his friend, staring wonderingly at him.

'Do I? O, I am so much better than I was. At first it was horrible pain.'

'But how did it happen?'

'I don't know,' says Cesare, looking puzzled. 'I remember nothing about it.'

'You were crossing Gray's-inn-road, were you not?'

'Yes, and there came a sort of crash all of a sudden; and I remember nothing more until I woke up in the most horrible pain.' And the child's lips quiver and his eyes fill.

'Well, we won't talk about that. What is that curious mound you have under the bed-clothes?'

'O, that is to keep the clothes from touching me, nurse said. Isn't it nice?'

'Well, I suppose it is. *I* never knew what it was to have too many coverings on.'

'Tell me how every one is at home?'

'O, well enough. And they are all so sorry for this.' He touches the cradle as he speaks. 'Old Simpole told me to say he would try and come to see you next week. Luigi is sorry too.'

'I don't care for *his* sorrow,' pouts the boy. 'I *hate* him!'

'Then you would not like him to come and see you? He told me to ask you whether he might do so.'

'No, no, no!' repeats Cesare fiercely; 'I will not see him!'

'All right; don't get excited. I say, Cesare, is there anything you would like to eat? I wonder if I might bring you something next time?'

'I should like some oranges. I am always so thirsty.'

'Well, you shall have them, if I can get them past that horrid old porter in the gateway. Do you know, he lays hold of everybody as they come in, and empties their pockets to see that they are not bringing in food!'

'How horrid!'

'I saw a woman come in just now with a little bag on her arm. "What have you got in here, ma'am?" says he. "Only a nice bit of cold plum-pudding for my little girl up-stairs!" she answers. "O please, sir, do let me take it to her; she is so fond of it!" "Nothing eatable is allowed to be taken to the patients by their friends," he growls. "Look there at the rules. I'll keep your pudding down here quite safe, and you shall have it when you come back."'

'Well, what was the end?'

'O, I did not stay to see. I came on in here.'

'Poor thing!' says Cesare, laughing. 'O dear! I must not laugh; it hurts me so.'

'Are you in pain now?'

'O yes, I ache all over. And I have such a pain all down my left leg!'

'Well, this is the last you will feel of it, at all events, for it will be gone to-morrow!'

'Gone *where?*'

'O, I don't know what they do with all the legs and arms they cut off.'

'O Beppo, what do you mean?' says Cesare, beginning to cry. 'Are not my legs under the bedclothes?'

'*Now* they are, of course; but they won't be there long. Why, Cesare, don't you know that your leg is going to be cut off?'

The child gives a hoarse scream, which brings the nurse to his bedside.

'Nurse, nurse, is it true that my leg has to be cut off?'

'You stupid donkey!' she exclaims, turning round angrily to Beppo, who stands thunderstruck at the effect his words have produced. 'Did I not tell you to say nothing about it?'

'*Dio mio*, I forgot!' ejaculates the unhappy Beppo.

'Get out this minute, sir! Leave the ward!'

'O, please, ma'am—'

'Do you hear me? *Go!*' and she points threateningly towards the door, until Beppo, crestfallen enough, slinks silently out.

Cesare has fallen into quite hysterical crying, and has to be soothed and comforted and fed before he can be left again.

Nurse inwardly vows to wage war against that imprudent chatterer of an organ-boy, who has so upset her little patient, and goes off into the next ward to fetch a soothing draught. Cesare lies quite still, with his eyes shut, exhausted after his long fit of sobbing.

Presently a soft whisper comes from one side of his bed.

'Cesare dear, are you asleep?'

He opens his eyes, and there is Beppo again.

'I thought you were gone,' he murmurs faintly.

'So *she* thinks,' returns Beppo, grinning maliciously, English anger here having proved itself no match for Italian cunning. 'I waited until her back was turned, and then stole in again. I could not go without asking you to forgive me. Will you?'

'Kiss me,' replies the child; and as the other stoops over him, Cesare feels a tear upon his cheek. 'O Beppo, will you do one thing for me?'

'Anything.'

'Go to Miss Haydon, and tell her that I am here. Ask her to come and see me.'

'I will.'

'Now go before nurse comes back. And bring me some oranges next time.'

'Would you like me to bring my monkey Pippo, too?'

'Not yet; when I am stronger.'

'Very well. Good-bye till next week. *Addio, poverino!*'

CHAPTER XIII.

ANOTHER VISITOR.

'VISITING-DAY again,' thinks Cesare, as he wakes out of a refreshing sleep on Tuesday morning. 'How long it seems since Friday! I wonder whether Beppo will come to-day? Perhaps Miss Haydon might come, if she knows that I am here. I hope he did tell her. Nurse,' he says, as a hot cup of tea is brought to his bedside by that functionary, 'when do you think I shall be able to get up and walk about?'

'O, in a few days, I daresay,' responds the nurse, who considers it her duty to take a cheerful view of life under all circumstances, regardless of truth. She knew that 'a few *weeks*' would be somewhat nearer the mark, but would not discourage him by saying so.

'Could I not sit up for a little while to-day, to begin with?'

'We'll see what the doctors say, my dear. You are a good little boy, and don't give me half the trouble that some of those men do; yet I daresay you are quite as tired of lying still as they can be.'

'O yes, I am tired of lying straight out on my back; and my leg hurts very much.'

'Well, I'll tell you one thing for your comfort. That very pain shows that your leg is growing and healing up, and so, perhaps, will not have to be cut off, after all. Look down there at the man in the third bed from you. He had an accident in some machinery that he was working, and was brought in here some days before you. Well, the doctors cut off his arm, but instead of hurting as your leg does, he has no pain at all —and he is *dying*.'

'Dying without pain! I thought it hurt so dreadfully to die.'

'Dying hurts less than living, sometimes, my dear. His arm is all mortified, gone to sleep, as it were, and he will never have any more pain in it; only he will never get better. His poor wife will come to-day, for they have sent to tell her that she must come and say good-bye to him. The doctor said last night that he could not live through the day.'

Cesare looks with awe at the man, who is

chatting unconsciously and gaily with his next neighbour, and tries to feel thankful for the sharp twinges which almost make him cry out every now and then. He counts over for the hundredth time how many hours must elapse before visiting-time begins; and then the doctors come in for their rounds, with the little knots of students, busy as bees, clustering round the beds, notebook and pencil in hand. He is learning to know them by name, and watches to see them come in, some brisk and busy and eager for their work, some abstracted and thoughtful. Little Dr. Bryon, who is always so cheerful and kind-hearted, though a trifle rough in his ways; and Dr. Morrison, the women's favourite, who listens so patiently to everybody's tale, and notes it all down in a brown-leather pocket-book; and Mr. Cardd, the surgeon, who looks as if he never heard a word you said to him, yet has the highest reputation of them all, as the most skilful operator in London, and who seems only to awaken out of a dream into keen activity at the prospect of any 'cutting up.' In fact, as Nurse Warren often said, he would hardly undertake any case in which there was not some 'cutting' to be done.

Cesare is Mr. Cardd's patient, and as that gentleman bends over him, examining his wounds, he trembles at the thought of what is before him, and longs to, yet dares not, ask if his leg is really to be cut off. However, comfort does come afterwards, for Mr. Cardd, however anxious he may be for an operation, is reluctantly compelled to admit that Cesare's leg is so much better that there is no present necessity for its removal; and Nurse Warren kindly tells the boy this, as she brings him his dinner. The sob of relief, which comes involuntarily as she pauses, tells how great had been his fear, and she bids him cheer up, for 'you shall go out walking as well as I do, after all, my dear.'

Two o'clock has but just struck when Beppo's round brown face appears at the door, and he advances with a triumphant smile.

'I have been waiting ever so long at the door until it was opened, and I've brought you two oranges; see!' And he pulls out the golden fruit. 'I held one under my arm, and the other in my pocket, and got through quite safely—'

'What have you got there?' says a voice behind him. 'Oranges? Did you bring them, lad? Yes, he may have oranges, as many as you like to bring, only another time you should ask leave.'

And Nurse Warren passes on, leaving Beppo somewhat discomfited.

'Well, I went to Miss Haydon, Cesare, and she was so kind and good, and so sorry to hear of your accident. She promised to come and see you this afternoon.'

'Peel me an orange,' whispers the child. 'I am so thirsty!' And Beppo strips off the thick peel and pulls the quarters one by one.

'Is it good?'

'Very,' answers Cesare, sucking away with infinite gusto. When he has finished, he piles the bits of peel into a little heap, and turns them about in his fingers. 'The last time I tasted an orange was at home,' he murmurs musingly. 'Nanna and I walked far outside the city till we came to some beautiful gardens—I do not know their name; and the orange-trees were laden with ripe fruit. We threw up stones, and they showered down upon us; so that we ate as many as we liked, sitting under the trees and looking out over the Campagna, with the river winding far, far away, and Rome at our feet.'

'Here is the lady!' exclaims Beppo, starting

to his feet, as Miss Haydon makes her appearance.

'My poor child, I am so sorry to see you here,' she says, as she takes her seat by the bedside, and touches his burning forehead with her cool soft hand.

'I am so glad to see you again, ma'am,' he whispers, looking up into her face, and feeling all at once comforted and protected. 'I have been thinking about what you said; and you see I nearly *did* die, just after your talking about it.'

'You will not die now, though, I hope, and it may be the beginning of a new life to you. Tell me; do you suffer much pain, and are you comfortable here?'

Here follows a long account of the past days' weariness and sufferings, poured into very sympathising ears, in the midst of which Beppo takes his leave, promising to come again very soon; and when Cesare has talked himself hoarse, he is regaled with another orange, his pillow smoothed, and his forehead cooled with a handkerchief soaked in eau de Cologne.

'I have not brought you anything to eat this time, because I could not tell what you would fancy; but you must tell me now, that I may bring it at my next visit. Is there anything that you would like?'

She presses him for an answer, and he presently owns that he has been longing for a thick slice of jam roll-pudding, such as he used to buy for a penny for his dinner.

'I am afraid nurse would not consider that very wholesome for you,' she says, smiling; 'but we shall see. Meanwhile here is something to amuse yourself with.' And she takes from her pocket a coloured picture-book.

'O, thank you, thank you, signora!' he exclaims with glistening eyes, as he turns over the pages.

'It is the story of *Little Red Riding-hood*,' she explains. 'Did you ever hear it?'

'No, ma'am. I never had a book of my own before.'

'Shall I write your name on it?' She takes out a pencil. 'Cesare—what? What *is* your other name, by the bye?'

'I have no other, signora,' he says, looking puzzled.

'What did they call you at home?'

'Cesare, Giuseppe's Cesare; that is all.'

'What was Giuseppe's other name, then?'

'I never heard any other name.'

'Well, I shall have to call you "Miss Haydon's Cesare"!' she says, laughing. 'Now make haste and get well, and be my little model again. Good-bye!'

CHAPTER XIV.

TWO LITTLE RED RIDING-HOODS.

The next time Miss Haydon makes her appearance she is not alone. Two little girls, in bright-scarlet cloaks and black-velvet hats, follow her into the ward, and look about them with shy eager curiosity.

'I have brought two more "Little Red Riding-hoods" to see you,' she says, as they come up to Cesare's bedside. 'Now, Janet and Nessie, open your basket and show Cesare what we have brought for him.'

The children seem hardly to recognise their former playfellow amid such strange surroundings. They take his hand silently, and proceed to unpack their treasures. First some bright golden oranges roll to Cesare's grasp, then a couple of sponge-cakes and a light jam-roll, a little packet of rusks, a pot of currant-jelly, and two more picture-books.

'We have painted these ourselves for you,'

explains Janet. 'We did not know what to bring you, and mother thought you would like these; so we have been painting them in our playtime ever since aunt Jane said she would bring us to see you.'

'We showed all the things to the porter at the door, and he said we might bring them in,' chimes in Agnes. 'Aunt Jane says we must never do anything without permission.'

'Aunt Jane is going to leave you here for a little while,' says Miss Haydon; 'so sit down by the bedside and talk, while I speak to nurse.'

And away she goes, wisely guessing that the children would find their tongues more easily alone. Nor does her surmise prove incorrect; for by degrees the merriment in Cesare's corner grows so loud that their aunt jumps up in dismay, declaring she must take her young people away.

'O ma'am, don't mind it,' says Nurse Warren. 'I am sure they are doing him good, and even the other patients like to watch them. Why, just that bit of bright colour in the room is refreshing like, and does one good to look at. I hope, ma'am, you will bring your little ladies here as often as you like.'

Miss Haydon thanks her, and promises to do so.

'We have got another little boy in the opposite ward, ma'am,' goes on nurse: 'he was brought in badly burnt two nights ago. If your young ladies could look in upon him, too, it would please him, I'm sure. He has hardly any friends.'

'They shall go, certainly. Perhaps I might see him now?'

'Yes, ma'am. This way. He is not burnt about the face at all, so it is not unpleasant to look at.'

And they cross the hall, and enter a smaller ward on the other side.

'This is little Harry,' says nurse, pausing by the bedside of a child, who lies stretched on his back with arms and hands swathed in cotton-wool. He is a pretty fair boy, with tangled golden curls and blue eyes.

'Why, what a wee boy to be in here! How old are you, Harry?'

But he is shy and tries to hide his face; only, poor little fellow, he is so bandaged up that he can scarcely move.

'He is four years old, ma'am.'

'And how did he manage to burn himself so badly?'

'Well, I don't know really. How was it, Harry?'

'Detting matches,' answers the child laconically.

'Ah, yes, that is often the case. Those little children are left all alone in a room—often even locked up while their mothers are out—and then, trying to reach something off the mantelshelf, their clothes catch fire. I heard of a case not long ago where a poor woman left her child sitting by the fire, and went out to buy some candles, locking the door to prevent his running out. When she came back, in about half an hour, she found a horrible mass of charred flesh upon the hearthrug; and that was all that remained to her of her child.'

'Dreadful!' says Miss Haydon, with a shudder. 'Well, little Harry, I will come and see you again, and bring you a nice orange. And now I must call the children.'

'Auntie,' says Janet, as she comes up to the bed, 'may I write a letter for Cesare? He wants so much to hear of his little foster-sister, Nanna, in Rome.'

'Have you never written since you left, Cesare?' says their aunt, sitting down beside him.

'No, signora. I could not write, so I thought I would wait until I had learnt, and then surprise her with a letter written all by myself. But now—now—' his lip quivers, 'now that I am here, and cannot learn any more, I should like to tell her that I am ill;' and two or three big tears roll down his white cheeks.

'You shall do so, my boy. Tell me what you want to say and I will write at once. Nurse, can you oblige me with a sheet of paper? I have a pencil, and will write it out fairly at home. Now begin.'

Cesare thinks for a minute or two, and then dictates as follows in Italian:

'Dear Nanna,—The time seems long since I saw you last. I have been selling violets and showing white mice in the streets; but I have not made my fortune, and some days ago I was run over and nearly killed. Now I am in the hospital, very ill, and I do not know what I shall do when I go out. Do not forget what we last said to each other, and pray for me.'

'I think that is all I have to say,' adds the boy, closing his eyes wearily.

'Well, how am I to end the letter?'

'How do you generally end love-letters?' he replies, with the utmost gravity.

'Is this a love-letter?' asks Miss Haydon, much amused.

'Certainly it is. Nanna is my betrothed; we shall marry by and by—when I am rich.'

Miss Haydon struggles to keep her countenance, while he proceeds,

'So, since you doubtless understand far better than I do the way to express all this, I leave it in your hands, signora.'

Miss Haydon thinks to herself that she will compose a suitable ending at home, and also add a postscript on her own account.

'Now for the address.'

Cesare had never thought of this necessary part of the epistle.

'I don't know it, signora.'

'What street do they live in? You surely know that?' she exclaims, rather impatiently.

'Via dell' Angele Custode' (the Street of the Guardian Angel).

'And the name?'

'Nanna.'

'Yes, yes; but what besides?'

'Nanna, daughter of Giuseppe the mason, and of Nita, his wife. Put that, please.'

'Well,' says Miss Haydon to herself, as she folds the paper and puts it into her pocket, 'this will be a curious epistle.'

All this conversation having been carried on in Italian, the two little girls are not much the wiser, and they begin to weary of their visit, and whisper one to another.

'How dreadful it must be to lie here all day with nothing to do, Nessie!'

'Yes, indeed; and such an ugly room. All whitewash and rafters; no pictures or even paper on the walls, and no curtains to the beds, and *always* somebody groaning in the corner.'

'I wonder whether there are any little girls here?'

'We might ask the nurse. Perhaps auntie would take us to see them another day?'

'They must be very dull, I am sure. Shall we save up some of our pocket-money and bring them some cakes and sweets next time?'

'Yes; let us do so.'

And they fall into a discussion over pictures

and dolls, and various old toys which might be mended up for the poor little children who lie all day long in bed, day after day, week after week, without a plaything or a book to help the long hours to pass. When Miss Haydon rises to go, they bid farewell to Cesare, and discourse eagerly all the way home on the most advantageous way of spending playtime and pocket-money for the amusement of sick children.

'What can we do, aunt Jane?' they ask; and she offers suggestions of scrap-books and dolls and little ornamental boxes filled with sweets, and various other small devices.

'If you will work well for the next three Saturdays, on Christmas-day you shall take a present to every child in the hospital; and I will take you also to visit another hospital, which is only for children, and very, very much in need of help, where all your little gifts would be gladly received. Let us see how many suffering little ones you can give pleasure to this Christmas; and I think, my dears, that you will find it the happiest Christmas you have ever spent.'

CHAPTER XV.

WHERE IS NANNA?

MEANWHILE what has become of Nanna since we saw her at the railway-station taking a last long look at the train which bore away her foster-brother for ever? The blank of loneliness is always heaviest to bear for the one left behind, who must henceforth go through the familiar round of daily work alone, missing at every turn the absent one.

Nanna went back to her flower-selling with a heavy heart. She chose Cesare's favourite corners to rest in when weary or heated with trudging through the crowded streets; and for a long time she ate her dinner every day on that fountain parapet where they had played together on the sweet sunny April morning long ago.

There is little difference in the minds of children between absence and death. Death to them is only a longer, a more hopeless journey; and it is no more to the child who hears how 'father is in heaven, and we shall see him again when we go there,' than it was last year when grandmother said that 'father has gone to India for seven or ten years.' It is all an indefinitely long time, immeasurable and eternal to them. So Cesare was, as it were, dead to Nanna. She could not picture him to herself, or fancy him, any more than if she had seen him lying dead in his little coffin and been desired to think of him as singing in the far-off blue heaven with wings and a crown.

Nanna was very unimaginative; and except vague notions of wealth and fortune she knew nothing of that far-off country beyond the seas to which he had gone.

So Cesare was dead—dead to her. He would never come back the same as he went— the little brown-skinned laughing boy with his long tangled black curls and lithesome limbs. Another Cesare might come to her some day, but not hers. And so she mourned silently for him as for one dead, and went about her daily life with a dull aching at her heart.

With Cesare it was quite different. He had left Nanna rooted in her home, and there he pictured her to himself when he thought of her.

He never doubted that she would go on working and selling and helping Nita, and dragging about the baby, for years to come in the same old round. He knew the streets she was walking along, and the turf where she plucked her violets, and the old frock which would by and by be passed on to Bicè, while a new one, made out of her mother's skirt, would take its place. He knew that when she came to be eleven or twelve she would make her First Communion, and have a white frock and veil and waxen taper, and walk in procession with other children amid an admiring crowd; and that mother Nita would be proud and happy on this one day, and caress her little daughter, and perhaps give a *festa* in her honour. And then all would go on as before, until he should come back and find Nanna a slim black-eyed maiden, and they would be married, and go and live in the dear old dirty street, and be happy for ever after.

He never dreamt of any change coming to Nanna. And yet, while he lies all unconscious on his sick-bed, the change has come.

It had been a wet autumn in Rome. Farther south the rains brought fearful floods; and later on the Tiber also overflowed, breaking into the poor houses on its banks, and leaving behind, as it retreated, the scourge of cholera.

One evening Nanna returned from her daily rounds to find mother Nita writhing in agony on her bed, and before morning she was a corpse. Twenty-four hours afterwards Giuseppe was attacked with the same fatal malady, and died with Nanna's hand in his, leaving her alone in that scene of desolation.

A kind neighbour took the baby. She had one of that age herself, she said, and she would keep it until the two girls could support their brother.

Bicè, who had run out of the house when her mother lay dying, and refused to return, was handed over by the authorities to an orphanage kept by some Sisters of St. Vincent; and while Nanna's fate hung in the balance, an elderly man appeared from a distant part of the country, claimed to be a cousin of the dead Giuseppe, and carried off Nanna to his own home.

So it came to pass that when Cesare's letter arrived, the postman, a new carrier, who did not yet know the people on his beat, inquired in vain, in the Street of the Angel Guardian, for 'one Giuseppe and his wife Nita.'

The women from the opposite house came out and said that they were both dead, and Nanna had been taken away by an old relative, they did not know were. They forgot Bicè in her orphanage—she had never been a favourite—but they guessed the letter was from Cesare, and wanted to open and read it. The postman shook his head, and said no, it must go to the Dead-Letter Office; and so it did, and in course of time found its way back to Miss Haydon's house, unread. And Nanna was in a new home.

How her cousin, or 'uncle Sandro,' as she called him, came to hear of her father's death, she could never ascertain. In all probability he had hoped to come in for a good sum of money, for he was evidently not over-pleased at finding himself burdened with a penniless growing girl. However, having put in his claim of relationship, he was forced to take the consequences; so on the morning after Giuseppe's funeral, Nanna found herself with uncle Sandro walking towards the very same railway-station where, some months ago, she had bidden farewell to Cesare.

She had already cried so much that no tears were left, and she followed the old man in a confused mechanical way, hardly looking back as they steamed away from the city. She had had no time to go to the fountain, or take a last look at all her old haunts, and her little head was bewildered and heavy with fatigue and wakeful nights and the sorrow and shock of their double bereavement. So she went down with him to his home in beautiful Sorrento, a fishing village near Naples, where the blue sea lay smiling under the noonday sun, and the slippery brown rocks were wet with spray as glittering as the handfuls the children had thrown in each other's faces in the Piazza di Spagna. And Nanna looked and looked again far out on the dim horizon, and strained her eyes to catch a glimpse of the land beyond, and fancied herself growing nearer to Cesare and England.

Old uncle Sandro was a bachelor and a fisherman; and Nanna kept his house, mended his nets, and went out barefoot every morning with a basket-load of fish for sale, trudging stoutly along the white dusty narrow roads with high walls on either side. And in summer-time she gathered wild strawberries and sold them to the visitors who drove past their door in great carriage-loads, laughing and scrambling in and out for flowers, or stopping for a drink of wine at the little inn.

She was very happy in this new home after a while. Uncle Sandro grew fond of her, and would call her his child, his daughter Nanna, and showed his gratitude for her care and devotion in many little ways. He gave her a gay kerchief on one *festa*, and a pair of silver earrings on another, and by and by a whole costume that she might be recognised for a true Sorrentese. Cesare, lying on his sick-bed in the hospital, as he dictated that letter, would scarcely have recognised his Nanna in the strong healthy girl standing on the shore, her clothes ruffled by the sea-breezes, her hair gathered into tight braids at the back of her head, as she shaded her eyes to watch the little boat tossing far away on the blue waves, and opened her fish-baskets to receive the incoming haul.

So the months lengthened into years, and no news ever came of Cesare from beyond the sea, and his memory grew dim in her heart. Only every morning and night as she knelt down to say her prayers, she remembered her child-love, and asked the dear God to bless him. And at first she used to pray that he might come back and marry her, that they might be happy together; and then she changed this to a prayer that she might see him again; and by and by she simply asked 'that he might be good and happy wherever he was.' Only she always kept safely folded by, in the little workbox uncle Sandro had given her, a faded bunch of purple violets, which Cesare had brought home unsold on that last day in the Roman streets together.

CHAPTER XVI.

CHRISTMAS IN THE WARDS.

CHRISTMAS-EVE comes all too soon for the busy little workers in Russell-square. There has been great discussion as to whether their visit to the hospital is to be paid on the eve or the day itself, which is ended by their mother's final decision in favour of Christmas afternoon; so at half-past two the children sally forth accompanied by aunt Jane, who has dined with them on a magnificent turkey, followed by the orthodox mince-pies and plum-pudding. The children are in high glee, and dance merrily along the streets, each with a basket on her arm, full of chatter and excitement.

'A merry Christmas to you, Mr. Porter!' laughs Agnes, as she hops across the doorway. 'Here is a Christmas-box!'

The porter grins and touches his hat, and the 'two little Red Riding-hoods,' as every one calls them, tap lightly at the door of the 'Accident Ward.' Cesare is sitting up in bed for the first time, in honour of the happy occasion, and his little face beams with gladness as they come up to him, uttering all sorts of good wishes.

'We drank your health to-day at dinner, Cesare, and wished that you might be quite well soon.'

'And so you will, I hope,' adds Miss Haydon kindly. 'Has Father Martini been to see you?'

'Yes, signora,' answers the boy, with a grateful look; 'he did come yesterday, and was so good and kind. I feel very happy now. Luigi came to see me too this morning, and we are quite good friends again now.'

'So you have gained the Christmas blessing of "peace on earth,"' she comments, laying her hand upon the child's head. 'I wish you had been well enough to come to church with us; that will be the next thing to look forward to.'

'You will soon be up now, won't you?' says Janet.

'Nurse says I may begin to get up in another week, Miss Janet.'

'That's right! Now look here: a picture-book and a box of soldiers, a pot of jam, and some more of these little cakes that you are so fond of, and a new cap for the time when you are able to get out.'

'And this is my present,' says aunt Jane, unrolling a paper parcel. 'A flannel-jacket to keep you warm, now that you are sitting up in bed.'

'O aunt Jane, that *is* a pretty one!' cry both children simultaneously.

Cesare looks from one to the other quite bewildered by the pile of gifts; then breaks forth into voluble thanks in his native tongue.

'Why who is this?' says aunt Jane, as a small boy trots gravely up to them with outstretched hands. 'Little Harry up and dressed!'

'Me want somefin too,' says the urchin, devouring the toys with all his eyes.

'I've got something for you, Harry. Come and sit on my lap, and you shall have it.'

And Harry submits to be dragged upon Janet's lap and well kissed, and presented with a gaily-painted cock, which nods its head and tail at the company, and a wonderful wooden man, who jumps over a pole and back again, to the child's intense delight.

'Tell us what you have had for dinner Harry.'

'Pum-pudden,' he answers, hunting in Nessie's pocket for sweets.

'And roast-beef,' adds Cesare, 'and oranges afterwards.'

'What a good dinner! And nurse has decorated the ward with greens quite gaily. O, by the bye, Janet, you have got something for nurse, have you not? Go and give it to her while I talk to Cesare.'

So nurse is presented with a pincushion made in a walnut-shell, and a needlecase from Nessie; and then they pass on up-stairs to visit and give picture-books or toys to three more small sufferers in the women's wards.

'What do you think of doing when you are well enough to leave this place?' asks Mis Haydon of Cesare, as she sits by his bedside waiting for her young charges.

"I don't know at all, ma'am. What can I do with my lame leg? Nurse says it will be a long time before it is quite strong again.'

'Well, I sent for your master, Giacomo, the other day, and had a long talk with him about you. Of course, he is legally bound to maintain you; but as he declares that you cannot work for some time, you would be a great burden to him. Well, I do not know what we may arrange; but I want to tell you that when you leave this, you may come to my house until you are strong enough to work. I hope, indeed, to get admittance for you into some Convalescent Home near the sea; but in any case, you may come to me afterwards. By the bye, how old are you?'

'Ten, ma'am. At least, I suppose I must be by this time. Nita said that my birthday was towards the end of the year.'

'I wish you were older. What with your small size and your lameness it will be very difficult to find anything for you to do.'

And the little girls having by this time returned, Miss Haydon takes them home, revolving in her own mind various plans for the future.

The first thing she sets herself to accomplish is sending him to the seaside; and little more than a fortnight after this Christmas-day, Cesare is sent off to a delightful house by the sea on the southern coast, where he has nothing to do but eat and drink and sleep and grow fat; and this he manages to perform so successfully that his kind little friends hardly know him when, after six weeks' absence, he returns to London and takes up his abode in Miss Haydon's house.

Here he has a tiny garret-room given to him near the skylighted studio, where the artist paints all day; and he learns to dust her easel, rub her colours, carry her messages, and make himself generally useful, with large margin of time for study.

'I cannot think why you burden yourself with that child,' observes a lady to her one day, as Cesare leaves the room on some errand.

'In the first place he is no burden at all,' replies Miss Haydon; 'he is most useful to me.'

'I wonder you can afford to keep him, though. I always thought you had not enough to live on yourself.'

'I find that I manage very well,' says the artist, painting away rapidly. 'You know how utterly destitute he is. I do not know that I shall keep him always, but I shall certainly put him in the way of earning his own living.'

'What do you intend him for?'

'I cannot tell yet. I must watch, and find out his "vocation." Meanwhile, he is going to school to learn "the three r's," that he may be fit for some occupation, such as that of amanuensis, or cashier in a shop.'

'But, dear me! just think what years it

will be before that child is old enough for **anything of the sort.**'

'I wish he was older, certainly; but that cannot be helped, and he is old for his age in mind and feeling, I assure you.'

'Well, you know your own business best, of course,' concludes her friend, shrugging her shoulders. 'I must say it is very courageous in you to undertake the training of a wild Italian boy out of the streets, who may be a thief and a pickpocket, and I know not what besides.'

'I am too poor to possess anything worth stealing!' laughs the artist, 'and I hardly think that old palettes and worn brushes would sell. You really must let me make the attempt; and if you say a word more I shall insist upon your doing penance by giving me a contribution towards his new clothes.'

Her visitor only laughs and goes off, saying 'Good-bye!' but the same evening come a note and a bundle, containing a sovereign and a worn, but still good, cloth suit, with these words:

'My dear Miss Haydon,—You are the best and most trustful woman I know. Although I abuse you, I admire you all the time, and send the enclosed sovereign as proof thereof, to be expended on behalf of your *protégé*. The clothes are some of my youngest boy's left-off garments, and if suitable, I think I can promise you some more during the summer. I only ask in return one proof of your friendship, viz. that when you are in need of help, you will let me give it.—I am yours sincerely, ANNA FORSYTH.'

CHAPTER XVII.

CESARE'S VOCATION.

So the days pass by of Cesare's second summer in London; the weary, long, hot days, when the rich are gone for their country rest or foreign travels, and the poor sicken with fevers, and the workers pant for breath in hot close rooms, yearning in vain for a whiff of sweet fresh air. The artist has to work harder than ever to keep herself and her adopted child; yet her eye is brighter and her step more light, and a new element of interest has come into her lonely life in the orphan boy who shares her little home. There is a good school near, which he daily attends, working in the evening with his kind friend so diligently that he has already caught up the boys of his own age in the third class, and bids fair to become ere long a candidate for the second. This is the way in which his days are spent. At seven o'clock he is in the little studio, dusting and arranging those cherished treasures which Miss Haydon will not trust to the care of servants—a few busts and statues and other nicknacks from Italy, and her painting apparatus. Then he looks over his lessons for school, while the maid lays the breakfast; and at eight o'clock precisely Miss Haydon makes her appearance, and the meal is eaten in silence. By nine o'clock school begins, and Cesare is always waiting at the door, book-bag in hand, before the bell rings. He takes his dinner with him, so as to enjoy a good game of play with the other boys between lesson-hours, and at four o'clock the little stream of boys rush joyously along the streets to their respective homes. Then comes the 'idle hour,' dear to Cesare's heart, when, excepting in the long summer-days, his mistress and he sit by the fire or at the window, and talk, and he is shown how much she has done since morning, and announces in his turn the results of that day's labour. And then they have tea together, and a long walk afterwards, or lessons and pleasant reading until bedtime.

Meanwhile some changes have taken place in the home at Russell-square. Mr. Haydon, who had been for so long an invalid, died in the month of June. His widow gave up the house and went to the south for change of air and scene, and their two little girls were sent to school in Brighton, with a promise from aunt Jane that if they were very good and diligent they should come and spend their Christmas holidays with her, and visit the dear old hospital again.

How proud was Cesare when he wrote his first letter to the young ladies! And how delighted when, a few days afterwards, a letter came by post, all for himself, addressed to 'Cesare Haydon'!

'Are you tired of lessons yet, I wonder?' wrote poor Agnes. 'I am, I can tell you. We have to get up at six o'clock and practise for an hour and a half; then prayers; then breakfast; then lessons all day long. Only half an hour's recreation, besides an hour's stiff walk along the esplanade, two and two, with a cross old governess behind, who calls out, "Hold up your head, Miss Agnes! Put in your chin, Miss Janet! Not so fast, girls!" until I feel almost tempted to jump right over into the sea, just to vex her. As for the elder girls, they are up at half-past five, working for prizes; but I shall never do that, so you may tell aunt Jane to give up all idea of ever seeing me come home with gold and silver medals and morocco-bound books. " The game is not worth the candle," as the French governess says.'

'This place is really not so bad as Agnes makes out,' wrote Janet. 'Miss Bevan is very kind ; and I do enjoy being with a number of other girls ; it is such fun having all sorts of games and dressing up and acting, as we do on half-holidays. Agnes is very diligent, too, though she would be quite angry if she knew I said so ; and the governesses are all fond of her. I must tell you something she said the other day, which I think would please aunt Jane. She had some German exercises to prepare ; and as we were all sitting over our lessons one evening, another girl came in who is very fond of Agnes. She went and sat down by her and looked over her book, and then she said, " O, I know all these exercises; I have done them myself. Let me help you, and you will finish them in no time. I shall translate them, and show you what the words mean, and you write them down." " No, thank you," says Agnes ; " I would rather do them alone." Minnie got very red and angry, and said, " O, you think yourself too clever to need any help, I suppose?" "No, I don't," said Agnes. "Well, you surely can't think it *wrong;* for if I tell you the meanings of the words it teaches you just as much as if you looked them out in the dictionary." Still Agnes did not explain, and I could not think what was in her head, and we all said, "Do tell us why you will not let Minnie help you." And then she said, "Well, you know I am always thinking of what aunt Jane taught us, 'Whatsoever thy hand findeth to do, do it with thy might.' If that is true, it means that we are to take trouble about things; and if I just wrote from Minnie's dictation, in a slovenly kind of way, without trying to do it by myself, I should not be 'doing it with my might,' should I?"'

'Agnes was quite right,' observes Miss Haydon, when Cesare reads this out to her; 'and you may go on the same principle in your school-work.'

'Then I suppose that is the reason why the use of "cribs" is wrong, signora?''

'That, and many others. It is deceitful—acting a lie, as it were—for you show as your own work that which is not your own, but the copy of another.'

'You cannot think how hard it is not to use them, though,' says the boy, shaking his head. 'The other fellows thrash one if one doesn't do everything that they do. They can't bear one to do better than they do themselves. Why, only yesterday I was thrashed for being at the top of the class.'

'How was that?'

'Why, when we were repeating our lessons, I got on better than the rest, and one boy, who was above me, whispered, "If you get up to the top, I'll thrash you when we come out!" Of course I went on all the same; but I knew what I had to expect, and I got it too!'

'Well, it seems very unfair; but I suppose it can't be helped. I don't know why it is that English boys seem to think so many kicks and blows are necessary before they can be men. However, all you have to do, my dear boy, is to be very brave and honest, and work with all your might.'

Cesare lifts her hand to his lips, after the pretty, impulsive, foreign fashion, and she bids him 'Good-night.'

'I wish, Cesare,' observes Miss Haydon one day, 'that you would give me some idea of what you wish your future life to be. You know almost enough now to begin work, I think.'

Cesare colours, and hangs his head without answering.

'Have you got any plan in your head?' she questions, looking earnestly at him.

'Wait a little longer, please, signora; I will tell you before very long.'

'I will wait if you desire it, and really have some good reason for asking it, my boy. Only remember, though I do not wish to make you feel under any painful obligation to me, that at present I am working for us both; and I am getting old, and labour is harder than it used to be. You will wish yourself, I am sure, to begin soon to earn money on your own account.'

The boy grows agitated as she speaks, and the colour dies away from his face.

'I will answer you soon, dear signora; indeed I will; only give me a little time to think.'

'Very well, I will give you a week. On this day week you must tell me your decision.'

And they speak no more on the subject.

CHAPTER XVIII.

'TO BE, OR NOT TO BE.'

ONE morning in the following week Miss Haydon wakes, as she thinks, at her usual time, and remembers that she has left her watch on the studio table. While listening for the sound of work down-stairs, her ear catches that of a church clock striking faintly in the distance.

'Four, five, six—yes, it must be seven o'clock. At all events, I will get up and dress!' she says to herself, looking ruefully at the empty watch-stand by her bed.

While dressing, she wonders at the unusual quiet, and questions in her own mind why the blinds of the opposite house are still drawn down.

'Am I very early, after all, or is every one else late, or what is the matter?' she says to herself, and going out into the passage she calls up-stairs, 'Mary Ann!'

'Yes, ma'am!' responds the sleepy maid-of-all-work, opening her door.

'What time is it?'

'About a quarter to six, ma'am.'

'Dear me, how stupid! I am an hour too early! What shall I do with myself now? I can't go back to bed again. Well, I must make a virtue of necessity, and do an hour or so of painting before breakfast.'

With this purpose in view she finishes her toilette, and ascending the stairs, opens the door of her studio and enters.

Hardly has she advanced into the middle of the room when she turns her eyes to the window, and stands rooted to the spot in mute amazement.

Perched upon a high stool before her own easel, maulstick and brush in hand and palette on thumb, intent on his work, sits Cesare. He is so absorbed that he does not hear her approach, so she steals softly up behind him and looks over his shoulder. He is putting the finishing touches to a picture of the Madonna, drawn from one that she had herself copied, long ago, in the Pitti Palace at Florence, and brought home to her little dusty London studio in memory of brighter days, when her own easel had stood among the crowd of those who strove to reproduce, ever so faintly, the divine sweetness of

Raffaelle's 'Madonna del Gran' Duca.' The boy's draughtsmanship was faulty enough, of course, and the most ignorant of amateurs would have found plenty to laugh at in the happy unconsciousness with which he transgressed the fundamental rules of perspective. Nevertheless, there shone out from his little rude copy, with its glaring reds and greens and its awkward foreshortenings, such a glimpse of true artistic feeling, nay genius, that his mistress stood speechless with astonishment and almost reverence.

With a long sigh, he at length lays down his brush, and slowly descends from his perch to take a good look at the whole. As he turns, he finds himself face to face with his mistress.

'Signora!' falters the poor child, growing red and pale by turns. His voice fails him, and he trembles with agitation.

Miss Haydon is the first to recover herself. She speaks very slowly and gravely.

'How long have you been painting here?'

'All the summer, signora,' he whispers, hanging his head.

'Who taught you?'

'I watched you, signora; no one else.'

'And where did you get your colours?'

'You gave me this old broken palette once to throw away, and the colours I collected when I cleaned your palettes.'

'And the canvas?'

'I bought it with the pennies you gave me for sweets.'

Miss Haydon pauses a moment, bending over the picture as though examining it. Inwardly she admires him, but is resolved not to show it.

'And what is to be the end of this, may I ask? Is it to help you to be a counting-house clerk or a shop-boy, or *what?*'

'Signora—signora!' he stammers.

'Speak out and tell me what is in your mind, child.'

'O signora!' he exclaims, bursting into tears, 'I want to be an artist. I do indeed! O, do not tell me to give it up!' he continues, falling on his knees before her. 'I love you so much; but I cannot—cannot do anything else!'

'And have you considered what "being an artist" involves? Seven or eight years' study at the very least before you can begin to earn anything; and who is to support you in the mean while?'

The boy looks up with a despairing appeal in his eyes, but does not answer; and Miss

Haydon begins to walk up and down the room with a grave face, rapt in thought.

'Look here, Cesare,' she says, 'I suppose that to-day is to be the turning-point in your life. We cannot decide this matter hastily. I will take a whole day's holiday, and we will go down to Hampton Court, and take our dinner, and have a long talk.'

'Then you are not angry with me, signora?' says the boy timidly, venturing to look up at her.

'No, I am not angry.' And she holds out her hand, which he covers with kisses.

It is a warm bright day in early September. As they leave the house silently, Miss Haydon turns her steps towards the church, and they enter and kneel down before the altar. Cesare remembers suddenly, with a vivid flash of memory, the morning when he knelt here, desolately weeping over his dead mice.

'O dear God,' he murmurs softly, 'do let me be a painter! I will not ask for anything more; I will suffer anything—only make me a painter.'

And then they leave the church, and go on their way—a long walk in hot and dusty streets; then the train swiftly passing out through miles of houses into the pleasant country; and finally, a sweet quiet rest under green trees in the great still stretch of meadow-land before the old redbrick palace. Cesare has been there more than once before, and he knows the treasures inside; and now, as he lies down and hides his face in the long cool grass, he wonders whether he shall ever paint such pictures, and come here some day with a right to look upon them as an artist; or whether all his dreams are to be ended from that time forth. He cannot bear to go inside and see the things which remind him that his fate is lying now in the hands of a woman—of that woman who has hitherto been almost a mother to him, but of whom at this moment he can only pray that he may not hate her if she shut the gates of his paradise upon him for ever. And as he prays, he feels her soft touch upon his head, and her voice telling him to rise and look her in the face.

He draws himself up slowly, with the traces of tears upon his cheeks. She looks gravely, tenderly down upon him, and thinks to herself that he seems to have grown older since yesterday.

'Do not be afraid of me, my Cesare,' she

says. 'Speak out like a man, and tell me all that is in your heart. Do you honestly think that you have the power within you which would make you devote your whole life to the study of painting?'

'I do, signora.'

'And you could not give up your days to work in other ways, and let painting be your recreation?'

'I want it to be my *life*, signora.'

'Do you know what that means for *me*, Cesare? That *I* must work for *your* bread, instead of your helping and supporting me; and that if I die, you will be left penniless upon the world, instead of having a comfortable situation provided for you, and perhaps a home of your own. It is very difficult, child, to earn your livelihood in the service of art.'

'I will suffer anything for myself, signora; only—you—'

'Well,' she says, with a long sigh, rising to her feet, 'you shall try. I will send you to a good school of art, and if they say that there *is* genius in you, God forbid that I should frustrate His purposes. You shall be an artist.'

'And so you chose, by way of a first attempt, the master before whose divine touch centuries of fellow-artists have thrown down brush and pencil in despair! Is it the "sublime impudence" of genius, I wonder, or the ignorance of a child?'

'I do not know, signora mia,' smiles the boy, as he lies at her feet and looks up at her with loving eyes. 'I only know that I looked until I loved it, and then somehow I took it down and began.'

'Will you have a name some day, I wonder?' she muses aloud, playing with his hair.

'I hope so,' he answers proudly, looking back at her. 'I shall see my pictures hanging as those are, for all the world to see.' And he points over to the silent palace, with its vast galleries of paintings.

'And what name will they speak when they ask for *your* pictures?'

'Cesare—di Roma,' says the child; 'for I—am a Roman!'

CHAPTER XIX.

'ET APRÈS?'

IT is ten years since we last saw Cesare, lying at the feet of his fairy godmother amongst the soft grass in Hampton Court Gardens. Ten long weary years, in which summer has passed to winter, and winter blossomed into spring; and every day the artist has toiled on, painting early and late at her little north-lighted window, high up among the roofs, that she and her adopted son may have bread to eat. And day by day the boy too has worked on, straining every nerve to perfect himself more and more in his art, winning prizes and medals and commendations from his masters in the art-schools through which he successively passed, and gathering bright hopes for the future.

Sometimes, as he grew older, and learnt to know the extent of the sacrifice which she had made for him, he would creep away by himself and fret secretly at being such a useless burden, and almost feel tempted 'to throw away palette and brush, and go out and sweep the streets, or do anything rather than 'live on charity,' as he called it to himself. But then she was so sweet, so sweet, that he almost felt how good it was to owe everything to one we love; and he said to himself, as so many have done before him, 'Only wait a while, and I will make it all up to her in her old age.'

'You are sad, my child,' she said to him one day, laying her thin white hand caressingly upon his head.

'Yes, signora mia, I feel sometimes as though I could not bear it. To go on living as I am, taking everything from you and giving nothing back. If I were your child it would not so much matter; but——for a *stranger?*'

'Do you give me *nothing* in return, Cesare?' she whispered, with a strange thrill in her voice; 'not even a little love? O child, you will understand some day. How I thank God that you have come into my life! I was lonely; I had never done any one any good. And now I have you at my own fireside to be to me as a son in my old age. And when I die I shall go to God, and say, "Behold, O Lord, I have done some work in my life; I have kept one soul pure and true and glad for Thee!" Never say or think again that you are a burden, Cesare. Only, when you are a man, if you desire to reward me, do for others what I have done for you. Save them from being sucked into the vast whirlpool of wickedness and degradation around, and draw them up to the higher life beyond.'

And he understood her, and was silent; and went back to his work comforted, yet awed, feeling as though his life were a sacred thing. No fulfilment of a common task, as others thought, but a sacred vestal fire burning up to God. *His* part in the great battle of life, which none but himself could play, in which none but he could win the victory.

So in these ten years' time the artist and the child have been all in all to each other. The slight weak form of the deformed woman is more bent, her hair more gray, her hand feebler than of old; but still she paints on; and her adopted son has grown into a young man of twenty, tall, active, and healthful, with a loving light in his eye, and a steadfast purpose in his heart. There is another easel in the little window, for Cesare has set up for himself, and is at work upon his first picture.

He sings to himself as he paints, now on this clear April morning, while his 'signora' peeps over his shoulder to examine his progress before settling down to her own work, and watches his bright, eager, earnest face with almost motherly fondness.

'That arm, Cesare, look; it wants a little more shading, does it not?'

'Let us see.' He throws his head back for a better view, tossing aside the curls which cluster over his forehead.

'Rat-tat, rat-tat! There's the postman. Any letters for this house, I wonder? Yes, I declare! None for us, at all events. *We* never have letters, do we, signora?'

'If your ears are so keen in hearing the postman, I shall begin to think you *do* expect a letter, sir,' she retorts playfully; and before he has time to reply the maid's voice is heard at the door.

'O my prophetic soul!' exclaims Cesare, jumping up, regardless of a small jug of water which he upsets in flying across the room. 'Roma, Roma, Roma!' he cries, reading the postmark and covering it with kisses ere he delivers it up to its owner. She, almost as excited as himself, puts on her spectacles and tears open the cover.

'What a long letter! From Agnes. Go on with your work, Cesare, and I will read it to you.'

'Well, I feel almost *too* excited to paint! Go on quickly, please!'

Miss Haydon reads:

'My darling Auntie,—It is such a long time since we wrote last, and I have so much to tell you, that I hardly know where to begin. You know how mother promised that after the amount of study we have been going through in Germany, we should have a nice holiday before returning home; and you may know also, as Janet wrote to you some weeks ago, how much we have been enjoying ourselves at the Lakes; though, as they say letters are so very often lost between this and England, I think it wisest to do, like M. Jourdain in the play, when some one asked him whether he knew what *prose* was, " Oui, mais faites comme si je ne le savais pas!"'

[Here follows a long description of scenery, &c., uninteresting to our readers.]

'When we had got as far south as Florence, which was the utmost mother intended to do, such a longing came over us all to "see Rome and die" (or perhaps "see Rome and *live*" would do equally well), that we came down here last week. And O, dear auntie, it is so splendid! We only want *you* to make it perfect. Could not you and Cesare come out to us for Easter? Give yourselves a holiday for once! Read mother's note, and then say "Yes."'

'Why does she tantalise one like that?' mutters Cesare, bending over his canvas.

'Let us see the note,' says Miss Haydon, turning over the envelope. 'O, here it is!'

She reads, and utters an exclamation of surprise. Mrs. Haydon's note proves to be a most pressing invitation for her sister-in-law and Cesare to come to Rome and be her guests at the Hôtel M. A cheque for 50*l*. is enclosed for travelling expenses; 'and the sooner you can come the better we shall be pleased, as the girls have set their hearts on having you here for Easter.'

When she looks up after reading this, Cesare's eyes are fixed upon her.

'Well?' he whispers, breathless with emotion.

'Would you like to go?' she answers, smiling.

'Like it! *Like* to go to Rome!'

'Because if you do, I see no reason why we

should not accept this kind invitation. I should much enjoy the holiday, and I think we have both earned it.'

Cesare springs up with a shout which rends the air, and causes the maid-of-all-work to fly up-stairs and burst into the room screaming 'Murder!' while the boot-and-knife boy runs into the next street calling for a fire-engine and the police. Their alarm is in no way mitigated at the sight of Cesare dancing a wild war-dance round Miss Haydon, with a chair in one hand and palette in the other, shouting himself hoarse with the intensity of his excitement, while she, no less delighted, implores him in vain to be calm and remember the lodgers underneath.

'I can't help it, if I'm turned out the next minute!' he pants. 'I am just mad with joy at the thought of going home.'

And the frightened servant departs unheard to lock herself into her room until the noise subsides and quiet reigns once more.

And so it comes to pass that Miss Haydon and Cesare pack up their slender stock of worldly goods, and set out upon their journey, leaving Cesare's picture to be exhibited, and if possible sold, before their return.

CHAPTER XX.

ANOTHER EASTERTIDE.

IN less than a fortnight after Mrs. Haydon's letter, Cesare wakes up one morning in a little white bed in a tiny room, and with dawning consciousness comes the thought that he is in Rome. He jumps up and looks out of the window, upon a very ordinary-looking street, somewhat sloping, and rugged as to pavement, and not over full of traffic. Still, it is Rome! He strains his memory to try and fancy that he remembers it as he dresses quickly and descends to the long public sitting-room. Some one is down before him, however; and as he advances into the room he recognises Janet, whom he had hardly yet spoken to, amid the hurried greetings of their last night's arrival.

'You are up early after your journey, Cesare.'
'O yes, I am longing to be out!' he exclaims,

eagerly. 'I was just going for a stroll before breakfast. Will you come with me?'

'Yes, if you will wait a moment,' she assents, gathering up a pile of maps and guide-books, and running up-stairs to fetch her hat and jacket.

They set out in silence, and Cesare glances shyly at his companion as they walk down the streets side by side. She has grown a tall fine girl, full of healthful vigour, and a great contrast to her sister, once the bright romping Nessie, now, alas, a pale invalid, though as spirited as ever. Both have fulfilled the promise of their youth in point of good looks, and are much admired: Janet with her soft steady gray eyes and fair smooth skin, with shiny hair neatly braided back; and Agnes shaking down long golden curls which will not be repressed, and the varying colour coming and going on her cheek.

'I hope you slept well after your journey?' inquires Janet, with due formality, as they turn the corner of their street and come upon a long 'piazza.'

'O!' exclaims Cesare, drawing a long breath; 'the Piazza di Spagna!'

'How do you know? How could you tell?' she questions, in surprise.

'I remember it,' he answers, flushing with emotion, and passing on with rapid steps. He leans against the fountain, and with the old childish impulse stretches out his hand to catch the water as it falls, looking up the steps where Bicè and her fellow-models used to sit. A child passes along at his side, in the familiar Roman dress, munching a bit of bread. 'Bicè! Are you Bicè?' he cries, catching hold of her.

But she pulls her skirt out of his grasp, and answers sullenly,

'No, my name is not Bicè; it is Margherita.'

'Where are they?' he thinks, his mind suddenly going back to those old forgotten days. 'Giuseppe and Nita, Nanna with her flowers, little Sandra and her wonderful "fortune:" where are they all?'

Janet rouses him from his reverie with an impatient exclamation. 'We really must not stand here so long. It looks so silly. People will wonder what we are doing.'

'*People!*' he flashes back at her. 'How can you care what people say—in Rome!'

She colours with anger. 'Very well, if you

will not walk on, I must return to the hotel alone.'

'I beg your pardon, Janet.' And he turns and follows her, remembering vividly that day eleven years ago, when he and Nanna had quarrelled over their violets just here, and then eaten white bread beside the fountain.

So they return: Janet in a huff, trying to appear cold and distant; Cesare full of old memories and yearnings after half-forgotten faces, fretting at the uncongenial companionship. After breakfast Miss Haydon and he stroll out together, so he is free to talk out all his thoughts.

'How I have forgotten them all, signora! I have hardly even thought of them since the day when my old letter was returned to me from the Dead-Letter Office. How is it that I have let ten years pass in silence?'

'It was difficult to know what to do, at such a distance,' she answers. 'We will do what we can to remedy it now, at all events. Suppose we go to the street where you used to live, and try to find out something of your foster-parents?'

'Ah, yes, let us go!' And they take a carriage from the nearest stand, and drive rapidly along the narrow ill-paved streets, dismissing it finally at the entrance of that well-remembered one which he had trodden for the last time eleven years since.

The houses seem small and dark and close, and Cesare is obliged to confess that he does not remember which among them is the one he once called 'home.' So they pass from door to door, and from room to room, asking vainly for 'Giuseppe the mason,' and none know the name. Every face is strange; not one remains who would care to see the orphan boy Cesare.

At length a woman, busy over her lace-cushion, looks up from a group of gossips clustering round a doorway, and says yes, she remembers the family. And she tells the story which our readers already know, of cholera, and death, and Nanna taken by her cousin.

'And Bicè?'

'Ah, yes, to be sure—the little one! She was sent to the good Sisters there in the next street. And the baby died.'

'Thank you,' says Miss Haydon gravely, glancing at her boy's sad face; 'we will go there.' And they walk on, and find the orphanage not far distant, with its cheerful red-brick front, and white doorstep, and a bright little Sister Porteress at the entrance, in her great white-flapped *cornette* cap and blue girdled robe.

She shows them into a tiny square parlour, with well-scrubbed floor and bare walls, and presently another Sister comes in.

'You have come to inquire for a child named Beatrice Lombardi?' she inquires, after courteously motioning her visitors to be seated. 'I regret to say that she is not here.'

Miss Haydon and Cesare exchange a look of disappointment, while the Sister continues:

'She was sent here by the authorities nearly eleven years ago, in 18—, and placed among the younger children in the fourth class. She was a restless discontented little thing, poor child; and after little more than two years, she ran away. I need not tell madame that every inquiry was made; but our search proved in vain. We have never heard anything of her.'

'My poor Bicè!' exclaims Cesare, with tears in his eyes.

'Yes, it was very sad,' assents the Superioress. 'She was so vain and spoilt, we could not get her to learn anything, and none of her young companions liked her. We tried to make her happy; but she fretted after fine clothes, and wanted to be a lady, and could not endure the school routine, and the gray uniform, and the rules of the house. Where she has gone, or whether she is still alive, God only knows. Poor little child!'

'We will not detain you any longer, madame,' says Miss Haydon, after a pause. 'Perhaps you will allow us to return another day to hear more particulars of her life here. I fear she is lost to us now for ever.'

'I fear so,' returns the Superioress, shaking her head gravely. 'Would you like to go over the establishment and see the other children? We have some here still who were companions of Beatrice, and would be pleased to talk to you about her.'

'Not to-day, thank you,' answers Miss Haydon. 'Another time, if you will allow it, we will visit the orphanage.' And they take their leave and pass out silently.

'O signora, they are all gone! Not one left, not one!'

'Ah, this is sad, indeed,' she answers. 'My heart aches for that poor lonely little child, who must have felt herself so alone in the world. If only you had written, Cesare, she might have felt that there was one at least who cared for her. It might have saved her.'

'But I did *not* care for her. She was always so cross and selfish to us. Nobody cared for her. You see she is absolutely forgotten even by those who remember the others.'

'Yet perhaps a little love might have made her better. Did you ever try to soften her heart with kindness?'

'O, don't speak of it now—now that it is too late! It will be a life-long sorrow to me, signora, that I might have done something to keep her from despair, and did not do it.'

'We will try and find Nanna then, at all events,' says Miss Haydon, striving to be cheerful. 'And now let us return to the hotel, where our friends must be wondering what can have become of us.'

By Mrs. Haydon's advice, the affair is put into the hands of the police; and while inquiries are being set on foot, Cesare, Janet, and Agnes give themselves most diligently to sight-seeing, until Agnes, the invalid, gets quite ill with over-exertion and excitement.

Miss Haydon then proposes that they should

take a run down to Naples, where sketching for the artists, and sea-air for the invalid, may be obtained with enjoyment for all. So to Naples they go, thus all unconsciously drawing near to the object of their search, and so fulfilling their destiny.

CHAPTER XXI.

WILL HE COME?

'Bitter is duty; bitterer were the love
Bought with the gold of duty.'   H. A.

IT is evening. A fair, calm, still sunset by the sea. Uncle Sandro sits at his open door, pipe in mouth, looking out in placid contentment, while his adopted daughter moves slowly to and fro indoors.

'Nanna!' he calls presently.

'Yes, uncle.'

'Are the nets spread out to dry?'

'Yes, uncle.'

'And the room clean?'

'Yes, uncle.'

'And the macaroni in the pot?'

'Yes, uncle.'

'Then give me my beretta, and I will go over to neighbour Tito for a chat.'

She brings him his cap and watches him

off, standing at the door in her sober brown working-dress and purple bodice, her slim fingers waving a mock farewell as he turns the corner. Then she returns up-stairs, and taking her workbox from its place, passes out through the window to a little flat terrace-roof which she calls her 'garden.' Here she has arranged a few pots of flowers, and trained a creeper to hang over her window; and she takes out a little stool and sits there with her work in her lap. She stitches away, singing gaily little snatches of the sailors' boat-songs, 'Stornelli' and 'Ritornelli' as they are called; telling of how the boat which is guided by love always comes safe to port. Ay, Nanna; and the boat of *thy* life is guided by a higher love than thou dost dream of as yet. By and by she needs another ball of cotton, and hunting in a corner of the box, her fingers close upon a bunch of withered violets. For a moment she does not remember them; then a flood of memories rises, and the tears come to her eyes.

'Ah, poor little Cesare!' she whispers. 'Where is he? Perhaps dead, or lost, like Bicè. He cannot have made his fortune, or he would have come back to us as he promised.' And she folds the flowers carefully in a piece of soft paper, and puts them away with a sigh.

Somehow the thought of Cesare has brought a great sadness, and she can no longer sing over her work. The fireflies come out as darkness falls, and little groups of children, playing in the street below, snatch at them with their hands, to carry the light into dark corners and see them burn.

Old Sandro comes in with half a dozen in his cap, or lodged in the folds of his clothes, which Nanna pitifully disentangles, and sets them free in the doorway to sail away once more into the blue darkness.

'Go, dear little "words of love,"' she murmurs—'go and find Cesare and Bicè, and tell them I have not forgotten.'

And then she comes in and sets the supper, and the two sit down to their plates of smoking macaroni.

'I met Pietro Bartolini this evening,' observes uncle Sandro, pausing over his second plateful of macaroni, and looking important.

'Yes; what did he say?' returns Nanna abstractedly.

'He asked your hand for his son in marriage.'

'Uncle Sandro, my hand! What did you say?'

'I said yes, by all means. I am very pleased at the whole affair, Nanna. Pietro is well off; his son will be very comfortable and have a thriving business (he already, as you know, shares my boat); and I shall only ask to sit in my chimney-corner and smoke my pipe in peace in my old age. Andrea is coming to see you to-morrow.'

'It is all arranged, then?' stammers Nanna, bewildered.

'Why, yes; we considered it so. You have no objection, have you?'

'It is so sudden,' falters the girl, blushing.

'Surely you knew it long ago, my child. Andrea's love for you is well known in all the place.'

'I did not think—' she stops. 'Do let me be free for a little longer!'

'Free! Good Heavens, what does the girl mean by "free"? Do you care for any one else?'

'O no!' she answers, shrinking.

'Well, well, go to bed now, and we will see to-morrow. Only do not slight Andrea when he comes. You will not get another such a husband in a hurry, I can tell you.'

So they bid each other good-night and part, and Nanna cries herself to sleep.

Why must this happy life change? she thinks. Why cannot she go on working for uncle Sandro and waiting for Cesare, and being happy in her own way? It was most unfortunate that she had come upon that bunch of violets this evening, on the very night of all others when it would have been better for her peace of mind if she had forgotten them and him.

She could not bear to give up the hope which had grown with her growth, though half unconsciously, that some day Cesare would return and find her faithful to him; and yet her strong common sense told her that she was merely wasting her young years for the sake of a most improbable fancy, and that, as Sandro often told her, it was as likely smoking Vesuvius over there should become a plain, as that Cesare would ever return. He had no idea that Nanna was in any way fretting after her boy-love. Italians, in spite of their outward demonstrativeness, are often exceedingly reserved within, and you may live for years amidst the froth of seeming expansiveness without knowing one whit the more of their inner lives.

Next morning, early as Nanna always rises, some one is up before her, and as she dresses a voice from the outside is singing gaily,

> 'E' salva la barchetta
> Guidata dal' amor.'

'There is Andrea,' she says to herself. 'I cannot avoid him. What shall I say?'

But she has no need to say anything. The young fisherman, lifting his red beretta as she opens the door, with a bow any gentleman might have envied, holds out a basket of fresh ripe red strawberries.

'I gathered these for you this morning, Nanna, thinking you might like them to sell. It is a fine day, and there will doubtless be many pleasure-parties passing this way.'

'Thank you, Andrea,' she answers brightly, taking the basket; 'it is very good of you, and I am glad to be spared the labour of gathering them.'

She looks up in his face so frankly that he, not being learned in the science of love, thinks that surely she loves him, and he bends down with infinite grace and touches her hand with his lips; then, turning, runs lightly down to the shore, where Sandro's little boat lies, drawn up high and dry on the shingle.

That day, as Andrea rightly surmised, there were plenty of excursionists' carriages passing along the white road before Sandro's house. Nanna puts on her large flapping yellow-straw hat for shelter from the sun, disposes her strawberries to the best advantage in dainty leaves and small baskets, and holds them out to the passers-by.

Towards evening, when her stock of fruit is almost exhausted, she piles up all that remains in a pretty open basket platted by herself, sticks a flower or two here and there, and stands at the door to await a carriage which she sees coming, heralded by a thick cloud of dust.

'This will be the last,' she says to herself, 'if only they will buy it. And then I can go in and prepare supper, and rest awhile before uncle Sandro returns.'

The carriage draws near, and she runs forward, holding up her basket as usual, and watching for a sign of assent.

Inside the carriage are four ladies; two young bright laughing faces, a widow in deep mourning, and a deformed woman. On the box a youth of about her own age, who leans back towards the others and laughs merrily. The two girls catch sight of Nanna.

'O, there are strawberries, real wild strawberries! Do let us have some; they are the first we have seen.'

And the carriage stops, and they stretch out eager hands for the basket.

'How much?'

'Twelve soldi, with the basket, ladies,' answers Nanna.

'How pretty she is!' whispers one of the girls. 'Would you not like to paint her just as she stands there now, with her pretty sunburnt face under the straw hat, and quaint costume?'

'Indeed I should,' replies the youth. 'I wonder if it could be managed?'

'Cesare!' calls out Miss Haydon from the other side, 'have you any coppers in your pocket?'

Cesare! The name strikes painfully upon Nanna's ear.

'Cesare?' she repeats, 'Cesare?'

She turns for a moment to look at him, in an agony of doubt, and fear and hope. Then, quite low:

'Are you *my* Cesare?' she murmurs.
'And you,—Nanna?'

No one ever knew what happened next. Somehow Nanna finds herself surrounded by a group of excited, exclaiming, laughing faces, and Cesare, her own Cesare, sobbing at her side. She had fainted for the first time in her life. Uncle Sandro, coming in soon after with his fishing-nets and his young partner and future son-in-law, stares in undisguised amazement to find four strange English ladies making themselves quite at home in his tiny room, while Nanna, on catching sight of him, sobs out,

'Uncle, uncle, he is come at last!'

Andrea has the good sense to lay down his fish-baskets and steal quietly away, unnoticed by any one; while the old man, quite bewildered, asks who and where is 'he.'

Nanna falls to sobbing again, and hugging Cesare, who is quite as much overcome as herself; so Miss Haydon comes forward and explains everything.

Uncle Sandro does not seem overpleased at the occurrence.

'What! Cesare, the lost Cesare? Not that

fine gentleman, surely? He has come into a fortune then, without letting any one know all this time.'

'No, signor, unfortunately I have no fortune. I am as poor as yourself; I owe everything, even my daily bread, to that good lady.'

Thus speaks Cesare, somewhat resentful at the implied imputation of neglect.

'I hope then, *Signor* Cesare, that you have not come to put any fine notions into my Nanna's head. She is a poor girl, but has been brought up honestly, and has not lived upon the bounty of gentlefolks. Moreover, she hopes to become the wife of a simple fisherman, who will not be over well-pleased with the idea of having such a fine gentleman as *this signor* for a—what shall I say?—adopted brother?'

'O uncle Sandro, pray be silent!' breaks forth Nanna, trembling at Cesare's lowering brow. 'Dear Cesare,' she whispers, 'had you not better go away now and come to-morrow again? He will be accustomed to the idea then.'

'Yes, that will be best,' assents Miss Haydon, motioning the rest of the party into the carriage. 'We will return about this time to-morrow.'

They drive off, and once more, after eleven

years, Nanna watches him depart, and turns from her window to weep tears of joy.

'So that is Cesare,' comments the old man over his supper that evening. 'Why does he come here to disturb our peace after neglecting us for so many years? What does he want of us, I wonder, that he brings his fine friends spying into our house?'

'O uncle Sandro, be just to him!' cries Nanna, striving to speak calmly. 'You know he could not trace me before; he says that he had tried and tried in vain.'

'I wish he never *had* found you!' growls the old man. 'Look here, Nanna. Are you going to turn round upon me now, and say you want to marry this Cesare? I will never give my consent to it, never! If you choose to leave the house which has sheltered you for so many years, with my curse upon you, do so. I stand in the place of a father to you, and I hope I have done a father's part; but I will *never* consent to your marriage with that fellow!'

Nanna grows white and cold as he speaks, but she does not flinch.

'Uncle Sandro,' she says, 'this is the first time you have ever been unjust or cruel to me; but what you say is true; you *have* been a father to me—and—I will never disobey you.'

She bursts into a violent fit of weeping, which cannot be controlled.

'My daughter,' he answers, speaking more gently than before, 'your word is always true. Promise me that you will never marry this Cesare.'

'Without your consent? Never.'

'And you will marry Andrea?'

'O, give me time!' she gasps out. 'Do not speak of that just yet.'

'Very well,' he answers gravely. And they speak no more that night.

The next morning she goes about her work as usual; but towards afternoon, from some vague unexplained feeling of respect to those above her in station, she arrays herself carefully in the Sunday dress, the pretty gay Sorrentese costume of which she is so proud, and sat thus at her door to await her visitors.

By and by they come—Miss Haydon and Cesare alone. The former had proposed staying at home; but Cesare had begged her so to accompany him, that she was fain to grant his request.

'But, Cesare,' she said, laying her hand on his arm as they drove along, 'am I to consider Nanna as your adopted sister or your bride, or what?'

'As my betrothed, if—if—she will have me,' he answers, blushing like a girl.

'Do you think that a wise arrangement?' she continues dryly. 'You, who are educated and refined, to marry a fisher-girl from Naples?'

'My birth is as low as hers,' he answers. 'Nay, more, I was taken in by her father out of charity. Could I be lower?'

'You have raised yourself to a position above hers.'

'Or rather you have raised me, signora.'

'True. Do you regret it?

'I! Never. Only it seems hard that I should be separated from her by the very thing which seemed so glorious and right and good in itself— my education.'

'You did not educate yourself for your own happiness, surely?'

'No. But, O signora, could not she be educated too?'

'It is somewhat late for that, I fear. Besides, is she not already promised?'

'She was promised to me eleven years since!' answers the young man fiercely. 'I have a right to claim her!'

'Don't interfere with any one else's rights, at all events,' she returns; and as she speaks, they draw up at the fisherman's door.

Nanna stands inside awaiting them, for she had gone in when she saw the carriage. Cesare bounds up the steps, joyous and bright, and Miss Haydon follows more slowly.

'My uncle is within,' she whispers falteringly. 'Had we not better take a little walk outside first?'

'Yes. Let us walk on the shore. We shall be quiet there,' Cesare assents. And the three pass out, and down to the waterside, where the little boats are drawn up, all in a row. Cesare is restless. He has so many things to say, and knows not how to begin; moreover, he is horribly puzzled by the complication which he had never before realised, of the difference in their respective positions.

'Look at that boat,' he says to Miss Haydon, pointing to one which a youth was pushing off to sea, at a little distance from them. 'He is going out for a sail. How nice it would be to have one too!'

'Yes, that is Giulio, going out with his boat!' says Nanna, noticing the direction in which he points, although he speaks in English.

'Do you think that he would take us out for an hour or two? We could talk so well at sea.'

'Certainly,' says Nanna, beckoning to Giulio to bring up his boat. They glide noiselessly along, Miss Haydon and Nanna side by side; the small bent figure, black-robed, and wan of face, with one hand clasped in Cesare's as he lies at their feet, and the strong rounded figure of the girl, bright in her holiday attire, her olive skin flushing deeply, and her two hands clasping and unclasping nervously as she looks down over the boat's side. Some moments pass before a word is spoken, then Miss Haydon breaks the silence.

'Children, I am very glad—you must both be glad and thankful that you have met once more.'

'O yes,' murmurs Nanna, with a sob in her voice.

'After ten years,' says Cesare, looking out to sea, and wondering how he shall get over his next sentence—'No, more than that—eleven, is it not? Nanna, do you remember the night we were last together?'

She puts down her hand to touch his without a word.

'Do you remember,' he goes on, with a great effort, 'how I asked, how we agreed, that when we met again, we should marry?'

'Have you thought of that through all these years, Cesare?' she answers, her dark eyes lighting up with sudden joy. 'You have not forgotten me, then, O *caro mio*. But hush!' she continues, as he is about to speak; 'it is very, very good of you, but it must not be.'

'You are already betrothed?' says Cesare, half jealous, half relieved.

'I am asked for, not bound yet,' falters the girl. 'My uncle Sandro, who has been a father to me, thou knowest, Cesare mio, wishes it to be so. He will not consent that I should marry thee.'

'And thou wilt not marry without his consent, I suppose?' Cesare rejoins, falling like her into the familiar 'thou' of old times.

Nanna shakes her head silently, the big tears gathering in her eyes.

Then I must be a brother to thee, as I was before, and give thee away at the altar to this more favoured suitor.' He laughs somewhat constrainedly as he speaks.

'If thou wilt,' says Nanna coldly, a dull pain at her heart. 'He does not love me, after all,' she thinks bitterly.

Miss Haydon reads on the girl's face the secret which Cesare so little guesses.

It cannot be helped, of course. The love, alas, is all on one side; but she will do what she can to heal the wound made by the boy's careless words. So she draws the girl's cold hand into hers with warm loving pressure, and tells of Cesare's childish griefs and later hopefulness in the years which they have spent together, showing delicately, and as it were by accident, how impossible it is that he should be otherwise than free from all that would hinder his progress in art and in his future career.

'He has to make money and a name before he can take a wife,' she says laughingly. 'And now, my children, we will leave the past, and look onward to the future. Nanna will soon be the happy bride of a brave fisherman, who has promised to shelter the declining years of her adopted father. Cesare must go back and work, work, work, in the smoke and fog of gloomy old London. His first picture being sold—'

'Signora?' shouts Cesare, in questioning delight.

'Take care, you will upset the boat. Yes, Cesare, I received the news this morning. It *is* sold, though not for any large sum. Still this is always a beginning and an encouragement for the future. So Cesare will go home and work, and by and by become a great artist. Then he will come back to Sorrento and paint our Nanna as the young Madonna, and it shall be hung up in the church here as a thank-offering.'

'And every one will say, "There is the great work of that distinguished artist, Cesare Lombardi di Roma—"'

'Until some one else asks, "Dear me, who is this Lombardi? I never heard of him before."'

Whereupon a merry war of words is carried on, and their laughter rings out over the rippling sea, until the Angelus calls from every bell-tower along the shore; the boatman stands bareheaded by the mast to murmur his evening prayer, and every head is bent for a while. Then the white oars dip again, the sail fills, and they are borne swiftly to the shore.

That night old uncle Sandro calls the neighbours in to drink the health of the newly-

affianced couple, Andrea Bartolini and Nanna
Alessandria Lombardi; and the next day the
whole English party leave Sorrento on their
way back to Rome.

So Cesare is an artist, and has his heart's
desire. He goes back to the tiny studio in the
close heavy air of London, and there, in graver
sadder mood, life begins in earnest for him. So
many days of early rising to catch the morning
sunlight, so many weeks and months of hard
work; sometimes meatless dinners that fresh
paints may be bought for a picture that, after all,
hangs unsold week after week at the dealer's, or
at last brings little more than the cost of the
material. Miss Haydon's own savings, accumu-
lating after years of toil, are carefully left un-
touched for an hour of sickness, and she herself
grows increasingly feeble. Cesare will not let
her do much work now. So she sits in her armchair by the window or fireside working and talking, sometimes giving a touch here and there to
an uncompleted picture. And so the time goes
by.

'Do you know, Cesare,' she says to him one
day, 'I think I am getting quite blind? Every-

thing grows so indistinct before my eyes. I can hardly see you now, and yet I can almost touch you.'

'Don't frighten me in that way, dear signora. I will have a doctor in to see you to-morrow.'

'I have seen one,' she answers quietly.

'Have you?' he exclaims, turning sharply round from his easel, and laying down the brush. 'What did he say?'

'He said—that it was true,' she answers, sighing a little as she speaks.

'That—you are going to be blind?'

'Yes; and that it is the beginning of the end, dear Cesare,' she says, coming over to him, and laying her hand on his.

'You do not mean that!' he cries, catching both her hands in his own. 'Signora—signora dearest, do not say that!'

'Why not?' she answers, smiling faintly, as she draws a chair to his side. 'I have done my work, I think, and put you into my place, and now—I want to rest.'

'But you can rest here,' he whispers, kneeling down before her, and looking up anxiously into her face.

'I can rest better in Paradise, *caro mio*.'

'And you will leave me here alone.'

'For a little while, dear. Just as I have lived here alone for, O, how many years! Do not cry, my Cesare. Think of what it will be to me.'

But he sobs uncontrollably, with his head on her knees, until she rouses him with a word.

'You must be brave for my sake, Cesare, or you will make me worse. Listen: I am not dying now, but the call may come at any moment, and you must be prepared as well as me. Meanwhile, for the short time we have left, let us be happy together.'

He rises, and leads her back to her chair in silence, and stands looking at her, stunned.

'Go on with your painting now,' she says, motioning towards the easel. 'You must finish that picture while I can see. It will be my last look at your work.'

After all, the call does not come so soon as they expected. Month after month goes by, and gradually Miss Haydon grows more and more infirm, while the dim eyes fail to see even her boy's anxious face looking so lovingly into her own.

Then one day comes the dreaded stroke—paralysis. 'This is the end,' she says, quite quietly, when the doctor has taken his leave, and they are preparing the little room for the last Sacraments. 'Come and hold my hand, my Cesare, that I may tell you what I wish to be done. First, you will write to my sister-in-law. She is in Algeria now, you know; you will find her address in my writing-case, with their last letters. Give dear Janet and Agnes my love. Poor little Nessie! I think she will follow me very soon, Cesare.' She stops exhausted. 'Give me a little wine. Now I can go on. Send my small gold chain to Nanna, that her baby Bicè may wear it some day and think of me. And for you, all that I have is yours. Not much to leave, but it will help you; and you will work hard, and be good and true, and remember that —I—shall—watch—for you—in Paradise.' She sinks back on the pillow and closes her eyes.

'I will, I will!' he whispers, laying her gently down, as the priest enters the room.

The service of commendation for a departing soul begins. Cesare, kneeling by the bed, sees a sudden light pass over her face. She raises herself from the pillow with wide-open straining eyes, and the faint voice gathers strength with a sudden cry,

'Yes—I am coming! I have finished—O Lord—the work—which Thou gavest—me—'

She falls back heavily on Cesare's outstretched arm, and the light is gone for ever.

And now how much of this little story remains to be told? Cesare is now in Rome, studying under an American artist, and bids fair to become famous on some not far-distant day. Nanna's southern home is happy and prosperous; her tiny Bicè and Cesare playing round her as she still brings out her fruit-baskets to the passers-by, looking forward to a visit from Cesare, who is to begin the great Madonna picture next spring. Mrs. Haydon and Janet have returned, sad at heart, to their old home, leaving a new grave far away in Egyptian soil; for the golden-haired Nessie has 'gone to auntie Jane in Paradise,' as her dying lips whispered to the sister with whom she had been one in life.

But not for long will they remain in Russell-square. One Eastertide more and then Janet, too, will be the wife of an English artist living in Rome, and so they will all be together.

Of Bicè no trace was ever found. Whether living or dead, that nine years' silence has remained unbroken up to this hour. Only Cesare, as he passes along the Roman streets by night, gazes often into the faces of the passers-by, or follows some street-singer with tattered garb and weary step, always praying and hoping that some day he may find his little unloved companion of childhood.

The grave where Jane Haydon's weary body rests is bright with fresh spring violets. One tuft, larger and sweeter than the rest, has been sent from Cesare in the Eternal City and planted by Janet, in loving tender remembrance of her who rescued and sheltered in days gone by the forlorn little street-seller of Roman violets.

THE END.

LONDON:
BOBSON AND SONS, PRINTERS, PANCRAS ROAD, N.W.

www.ingramcontent.com/pod-product-compliance
Lightning Source LLC
Chambersburg PA
CBHW020917230426
43666CB00008B/1477